PRAISE FOR ROLAND BARKSDALE-HALL

"This Guide OFFERS AN INTERESTING AND CREATIVE PATH FOR FAMILIES TO FOLLOW IN TRACING THEIR FAMILY'S ROOTS and (helps us) gain greater understanding and knowledge of our families using among other methods, the art of quilting and storytelling. This book should be one of every family's top ten books found in the home."
—Andrew P. Jackson, President
Black Caucus of the American Library Association

"Thank you to Roland Barksdale-Hall for daring to open a door within the black community that has remained closed for far too long — and beginning a conversation, that ends the deafening silence. Mr. Barksdale-Hall's love for HISTORY, AND REVERENCE FOR THE BLACK FAMILY IS BREATHTAKING as he guides us through the delicate lessons of knowing...knowing the good, and the not so good of Black America's rich history."
—Janis F. Kearney, former Diarist for President Bill Clinton
Author, Cotton Field of Dreams: A Memoir

"Roland Barksdale-Hall has produced a provocative and interesting guide to black genealogy that should be in every African American household."
—Eric Ledell Smith, Associate Historian
Pennsylvania Historical and Museum Commission

An important resource and guide for all African Americans.
—Bill Cosby

D1081880

.... "*a wonderful pathway to gaining a better understanding of ourselves, our families and our shared history. The book is a comprehensive guide that has the potential to be a must-read for years to come—not only for African Americans, but also for all those interested in family history. Understanding family history has helped inform some of my most important work—I only wish Mr. Barksdale-Hall's book would have been available to me some years ago when I began my journey.*"

> —Philip S. Hart, Ph.D., award-winning author, *Bessie Coleman: Just the Facts* and Co-owner, Tanya Hart Communications, Inc., (Hollywood, CA)

"*Roland Barksdale-Hall's appreciation for the past of our ancestors has helped him to write* ONE OF THE MOST IMPORTANT BOOKS FOR AFRICAN AMERICAN FAMILY RESEARCH. *He understands the important of trying to walk in the ancestors' shoes, providing himself with insights into their world that most researchers miss*".

> —Harry Bradshaw Matthews
> Executive Director, United States Colored Troops Institute
> Associate Dean at Hartwick College

"A real healing, resourceful, uniting, and family celebration. Roland Barksdale-Hall *incorporates the meaning and feelings of the African-American family in a holistic way.*"

> —Vandella Brown, author
> Celebrating the Family: Steps to Planning a Family Reunion

We all have these wonderful stories from the ordinary, yet mighty people, who have shaped our lives. Hopefully, you will be inspired by the works of Roland Barksdale Hall, and (you) **will be moved to begin your own journey (to find them)**.

> —Angela Y. Walton-Raji

"CULTURAL NUANCES... PERMEATE THIS BOOK."
—American Libraries

"Barksdale brings collective healing to us all. His work nurtures the spirit of Africa throughout the Diaspora."
—Rufus Tiefing Stevenson, MA,
Africanist & Curator, The Tiefing Collection, Inc.
Executive Vice President, Jah Kente International, Inc.

"As we prepare to meet the challenges of the 21st century, it is important to me that I know the thoughts and experiences of people who care about the future of America and the world. I am confident that, working together, we can protect our shared values and meet our common challenges."
—William Jefferson Clinton

The African American Family's Guide To Tracing Our Roots

Healing, Understanding & Restoring Our Families

by Roland Barksdale-Hall, MLS, MLLS, MA

The African American Family's Guide To Tracing Our Roots

Healing, Understanding & Restoring Our Families

by Roland Barksdale-Hall, MLS, MLLS, MA

Amber Books

Phoenix
New York   Los Angeles

THE AFRICAN AMERICAN FAMILY'S GUIDE TO TRACING OUR ROOTS: Healing,
Understanding & Restoring Our Families

by Roland Barksdale-Hall, MLS, MLLS, MA

Published by:
Amber Books
A Division of Amber Communications Group, Inc.
1334 East Chandler Boulevard, Suite 5-D67
Phoenix, Z 85048
amberbk@aol.com
WWW.AMBERBOOKS.COM

Tony Rose, Publisher/Editorial Director   Samuel P. Peabody, Associate Publisher
Yvonne Rose, Associate Publisher   Jannie M. Lathan, Associate Publisher
The Printed Page, Interior & Cover Design

AMBER BOOKS are available at special discounts for bulk purchases, sales promotions, fund raising or educational purposes.

ISBN#: 978-0-9749779-7-3

Library of Congress Cataloging-in-Publication Data
Barksdale-Hall, Roland C.

   The African-American family's guide to tracing our roots : healing, understanding & restoring our families / by Roland Barksdale-Hall.
    p. cm.
  ISBN 0-9749779-7-7 (pbk.)
  1. African American families. 2. African Americans—Ethnic identity. 3. African Americans—Social conditions. 4. African Americans—Genealogy. 5. African Americans—Life skills guides. I. Title.
  E185.86.B3725 2005

  929'.1'08996073—dc22

2005043662

Dedication

*To those who struggled and endured and to future generations
of free people to follow.*

*To my gifted young people, Colbert, Timothy, Imanuel,
Celeste, Therese, William, Jason, Vicente, Charity, Angelo,
Rillis, Demetrius, Drew, Alafasi, Shimannee, Adenugbe,
Vonita, and Imanuel-Tiefing*

Acknowledgments

Each one reach one, each one teach one

I would like to thank God for a vision and special people. Tony Rose, publisher of Amber Communications, for creating a space for folks to share their stories and Yvonne Rose, the best editor in the world. My mentor Sara Dillard Austin, charter member of the Western Pennsylvania African American Historical and Genealogical Society, Pittsburgh, who shared waffles and stories from her family. Karim Aldridge Rand, President of the H-Town AAHGS, Houston, and Robert H. Williams, co-founder of the International Sons and Daughters of Slave Ancestry, Chicago; who shared family stories along with research methodologies.

Salvador B. Waller, former director of the Howard University Health Sciences Library, who provided exposure to biomedical informatics. Charles L. Blockson and Haki R. Madhubuti, who have inspired me again and again with their scholarship and profound love of Black people. Dr. Laurence Glasco and Professor Wendell Wray, both of the University of Pittsburgh, who served as my faculty mentors. The first draft of this book represented a scholarly research project at the University of Pittsburgh.

Hampton University, my home by the sea, and colleagues at the William R. and Norma B. Harvey Library and Peabody Special Collection, in particular Gladys Smiley Bell, Cora Mae Reid, and Antoinette Carrington Tubbs, where plenty of inspiration and support came for bringing this work to completion. And to my Hampton hostess and friend, Barbara Holley, who provided a quiet atmosphere for reflection and writing.

Genealogists Sylvia Cooke Martin, past president of the AAHGS, Jean Sampson Scott, and Agnes Kane Callum, who saw a gift in me, recruited me to present my findings and later serve on the national board of the Afro-American Historical and Genealogical Society (AAHGS), Washington, D.C. Gladys Nesbit, who co-founded along with the author the Western Pennsylvania African American Historical and Genealogical Society, today known as the Pittsburgh AAHGS. Helen Fielder Comer, Addie Harris, Thelma Strong Eldridge, Carrie Kellogg Ray, Charles Barksdale, Richard Jackson, Ernest Fielder, Dillard Fielder, Mary Waters Stevenson, Gus Steverson, Ola Hudson Hester, Dorothy Steverson Malloy, Raymond Steverson, Mary Alice Ware, June P. Dowdy, Laverne Hunter, Ida Mary Lewis, Bessie Matthews Martin, and Mary Jane Katzman, who were valuable resources.

African American Genealogical Society of Cleveland, Ohio (AAGS) in particular past president, Dr. Deborah Abbott, for sponsoring helpful trips to research facilities of which I gratefully have joined. Pennsylvania State University for a faculty research grant that supported this project. Pat Newland, Tracie Hood and Nikki Marquis, who typed various versions of the manuscript. And last but not least Drusilla, Rillis, Drew, Vonita, Imanuel-Tiefing, Veronica, William, Shimannee, Demetrius, and my Cedar Avenue family for their steadfast love and devotion.

—R. Barksdale-Hall

About the Author

Roland Barksdale-Hall, founder of the Afro-American Historical and Genealogical Society (AAHGS) of Pittsburgh and executive director, has been researching the black family for more than 25 years. In 2004 he hosted a three-day healing family gathering, entitled "The Restoration of the Family." His research resulted in the Millennium Family Reunion, held in Detroit, bringing together more than 300 descendants of enslaved African ancestors. He has signed entries on the "Black Family in the Colonial Era" and "Inheritance and Slave Status" in the *African-American History Reference Series*, edited by Paul Finkelman (Oxford University Press, 2005). His intriguing family history has been showcased in an exhibition, "From Color To Culture" in New York. He is the recipient of the prestigious 2003 Afro-American Historical and Genealogical Society (AAHGS) National History Award and the former Peabody Special Collection Librarian, Hampton University, Hampton, Virginia.

He currently serves as president of JAH Kente International, Inc. and vice president of Black Men for Progress. He is the director of the Mercer County Junior Frontiers. He has served as the vice president of *The Buckeye* Review and on the executive committee of the Black Caucus of the American Library Association, Inc. Other professional memberships include International Sons and Daughters of Slave Ancestry, National Association of Black Storytellers and Mercer County Historical Society. His family is the recipient of the 2001 Women in Ministry Shenango Valley Christian Family Award.

Contents

Introduction

The self-help guide *The African-American Family's Guide to Tracing Our Roots Healing, Understanding, & Restoring Our Families* specifically is written in hope that we might rethink past events, explore vital health matters, and better understand our families. We share tips for researching roots, reconnecting with our past, and revitalizing families throughout *The African-American Family's Guide to Tracing Our Roots Healing, Understanding, & Restoring Our Families*. The healing art of storytelling is employed to provide lessons for analysis and dialogue. Second, it recalls our strong oral tradition. Meanwhile it calls us all to be an example and practice what we teach. *The African-American Family's Guide's* focus is to increase our level of awareness about cultural and historical identities and to develop better understanding of the events which helps to shape our families' values, beliefs, and attitudes.

Gaining knowledge is the first step in restoration. Discussion about ailments that run within families, how to request a death record, and identify the cause of death is included. We examine health and hereditary aspects of genealogical research along with health disparities of African Americans and changing destructive behavior.

We honor our ancestors and reflect upon twelve African traditions:
   ▼ God's omnipotent, omniscient, and omnipresent;
   ▼ Virtue of motherhood;
   ▼ Strong extended family ties;
   ▼ Disciplined living;
   ▼ Respect for elders;
   ▼ Ancestral land in perpetuity
   ▼ Transmission of knowledge;

▼ Significance of the arts;
▼ Sexual division of labor;
▼ Value of interpersonal and spiritual relationships;
▼ Rites of passage
▼ Sharing, caring, and honoring.

Our restoring work calls upon a critical eye for analysis of past and present events. The book looks at the destructive process of making of a slave, how slave status and inheritance, and race bating negatively impacted African-American families.

The African-American Family's Guide to Tracing Our Roots Healing, Understanding, & Restoring Our Families offers solutions. The self-help guide asks tough question in the Life Applications to provoke constructive thought and discussion. There are no right answers or wrong ones, though we respectfully call for thoughtful consideration. Our insights, which occur as we read, can be stored in "Our Great Ideas Notebook," which simply can be a plain notebook with lines or a blank journal for later reflection or group discussion. The book offers a twelve-step plan to health, wealth, and success.

▼ Practice conversion,
▼ Bond to healthy communities,
▼ Get our dollars to work,
▼ Rap with our elders,
▼ Join together for the common good,
▼ Vote in local, state, and national elections,
▼ Read more, increasing our cultural awareness,
▼ Know our history and rethink our past,
▼ Take a calculated risk, pursue our passion and birth a vision,
▼ Build bridges to confidence, unity,
▼ Celebrate life's passage and instill positive values,
▼ Excel in what we do.

The African-American Family's Guide to Tracing Our Roots Healing, Understanding, & Restoring Our Families recalls the heroic work of freed persons, who sought to nurture African-American families. *The*

African-American Family's Guide is a call to healthy relationships. We honor the commitment of loving, devoted freed people, who submitted out of love rather than fear and gave us five core values.

▼ An education takes folks somewhere,

▼ Stewardship of the land,

▼ Sharing, as expressed through a devotion to family, neighbors, and community,

▼ Commitment to the development of a viable African-American church; sacred and secular institutions,

▼ Hallmark of industry, as shown through a willingness to work hard and save, realizing every vision of God holds a fresh, revitalizing promise.

The self-help guide is a call to fetch back what is lost. *The African-American Family's Guide to Tracing Our Roots Healing, Understanding, & Restoring Our Families* is a call to get "love power" back to work. *The African-American Family's Guide* is a call to heal ourselves, seek restoration of families, and return to the way of caring and sharing.

—Roland Barksdale-Hall

Chapter One

Precious Keepsakes

Do you, like so many others feel like something is missing, perhaps desire to get the twinkle back into your eyes? To trace your family roots just might do the trick. It has put the twinkle back into my eyes and many others'.

My Grandma Mamie's devotion to what was her time honored handiwork of patchwork quilting has been recalled, time and again along my quest on the trail of elusive ancestors. To reflect all the more on what her legacy of cutting, tacking, and mending has meant, as I became all the more passionate about the search for my roots, albeit my healing tree, led to my scrawling a tribute poem.

Crazy Quilt
(for Grandma Mamie Steverson)

Birthday came
C R AZ Y QUI L T on the bed, lined with
throw-rug.
Purples of sister's frock, settling there;
I hear these patchessss:
Crying for me, telling corny jokes, saying
Hushshshsh BE STILL.
Papa's green flannel, removed from work-shirt must,
Pats me on the head.
Maroon and gold, brother's ugly plaid,
Snuck in, wrestles me to bed.
Orange criss-crosses, that's Momma's apple pie,
Topped with french vanilla borders
And laced coconut beneath:
Delights of saucer-filled eyes,
*   Coaxing, "sleeeeeeeeeeeeeeep."*

"Grandma's craft,"
 Sister tells me;
 Of course . . . ,
 Now I can see.
 Homespun snowflakes,
 Yessss that's Grandma,
 Like rocky-road, turtles, praline,
 Grandma whispers, "My Momma shows me how, with thread
 To pluck lovely chords, dashes of homespun
 To turn houses into homes, pieces of scrap,
 Don't you, don't you, DON'T YOU throw away,
 Gives them to me. I knows the way.
 Leaning over
 Good night kisses mixes of goooood things,
 Servings of vanilla sandwich cremes,
 Dips of Bruton Scotch snuff,
 I hears the spittle's ting
 Against Hills Brothers' shredded can,
 Lilac (soap) fills the room.
 Grandma's presence is
 Acceptance on failure-ridden days.
 I feels those hands, warming me,
 Saying, "boy, doooooooooos yo best."

Today, I continue to attempt to stand tall, upholding Grandma's charge, all the while rethinking what it has meant to be a recipient of one of Grandma's heirloom quilts. Grandma Mamie Steverson (nee Fielder) devoted countless hours of enjoyment to her patchwork quilting projects. Her project, begun with remnants of what might have been deemed "ready for discard," yielded an enormity of textures, contours, colors, sizes, and patterns. Finally, when Grandma's work appeared complete, there were always pieces remaining for the next project, which she folded away patiently, and awaited her tacking to a new backing.

Parallels exist between my Grandma Mamie's heirloom quilting and tracing your roots, as you too can expect guaranteed countless hours of enjoyment tracing your family roots. You, too, can expect a project inevitably set to mushroom with puzzle pieces (somewhat mind boggling at times) for every family member to get involved.

You likewise can expect to tack your work, remembering no piece of information will be great or small, on a backing—yours will be set on a multiethnic historic tapestry. You, too, can sense personal satisfaction in folding away the charts, notebooks, and clues only to await the moment that you can return.

Finally, your family too will beam, when they become proud recipients of your heirloom work of art, your family history, to be treasured for generations to come.

Gifts from the Heart

The televised drama Alex Haley's *Roots*, likely prompted the timing of my mother's legacy gift from the heart. Alex Haley's *Roots*, which traced the history of a black family beginning with its African progenitor Kunta Kente, aired to wide public acclaim in the 1970s. It was at the same time my mother in essence introduced me to our slave ancestor.

The introduction may have gone Barksdale this is your Great Grandfather Wilson Stevenson, a former slave. Well that is if my ancestor had not come of age almost six score and ten years ago. Alex Haley's family saga generated considerable attention, as evidenced by a rise in popular interest about the black family and genealogical organizations across the United States. The long shadow of slavery, as evidenced in *Roots*, had fallen on our sleepy little community.

It was in front of Grandma Mamie's mohagany-stained oak bureau and library acquired through her Larkin subscription sales that my mother's weathered almond hand touched mine pressing into my hand a clipping and implored.

> —Keep and preserve this memento.

The somber moment was to be etched in my memory and played over and over again, as it was shortly thereafter after both my parents passed within a few years of each other. I still can recall at that particular moment things rushing through my head. Why in the world had I not seen the mysterious keepsake before, my mother now held out, which was passing from one generation to the next?

Why he doesn't look much like a slave, I thought. He looks prosperous.

Before I put up the precious keepsake I stole another furtive glance— near the bust of a warm, round-faced, hearty well-manicured gentleman 1947 was scrawled. It was prior to *Roots* that my father sowed into my life a multi-volume set on Black history and literature, which he purchased for me as a gift through *Crisis Magazine*. All I knew then was that things were happening faster than I was accustomed.

Stevenson Millenium Family Reunion

Recently, I was thrilled to tell my family's story to several hundred people, the largest gathering of the Kellogg/Stevenson/Steverson family in more than a century. The family reunion was an outgrowth of the genealogical research for my book.

Stevenson Millenium Family Reunion Banquet Menu

Salads
Creamy Cole Slaw
Garden Salad Bowl
Pasta Salad Vinaigrette

Entrees
Sliced Roast Beef & Gravy
Glazed Honey Ham

Side Dishes
Mixed Vegetables
Redskin Potatoes
Buttered Noodles
Rice Pilaf

Warm Rolls and Butter
Chef's Assorted Dessert Display
Coffee, Tea and Milk

Special Photo Cake of Ancestors

Stevenson Millenium Family Reunion Program
Family Prayer

Father, in the name of Jesus, we thank you that you have poured your spirit upon our family from on high. Our wilderness has become a fruitful field and we value our fruitful field as a forest. Our family dwells in a peaceful place O Lord be gracious to us. Be our strength and defense. Father, we thank you for our peace, our safety, and welfare.

Program

Libation	Rufus Tiefing Stevenson, Former Second Secretary United States Embassy in London
Motivational Hymns	
Inspirational Poem	Ida Stevenson Poet
Stevenson Family History	Roland Barksdale-Hall Historian and Genealogist
Redemption Ritual	Diane Sommerfield Actress from "Days of Our Lives" and Rufus Stevenson
Acknowledgment of Graduates	
Special Awards	Stephanie R. Stevenson Chairperson/Organizer Mistress of Ceremonies
Time of Sharing	Family

Healing is the Children's Bread: Complete with the Holistic Health Guide. Bringing together descendants of fourteen brothers and sisters, who were slaves on a Stephenson plantation in Newnan, Georgia, and experienced separation, simply was a joy. People's eyes filled with tears as some rekindled friendships and others met for the first time.

I reminded the family however, in our jubilation to not forget our lost tribes who were not there. The family reunion's message underscored how despite our ancestors' selection of multiple surnames—Steverson, Stevenson, Brewster, and Kellogg—in slavery's aftermath, we shared a common legacy.

In keeping with the theme, "Reclaiming Our Past to Insure Our Future," we saluted the elders, who sat the children at their feet and trained them in what was the good and acceptable way. Our interconnectedness was dramatized in joining in a circle, tying kente strips together, and lifting the single chord over our heads. The synchronized motion symbolized our perpetual bonds of fidelity and love.

The twinkle now was back in my eyes. At that particular moment the realization that I perhaps had been chosen as the keeper of ancestral lore years ago now was beginning to jell with me.

My eyes shone just even a little brighter upon the thought of my Great Grandfather Wilson Stevenson, who took great stock in leaving us a Godly legacy. I peered around the Stevenson Millenium Reunion banquet facility arrayed in sashes of kente cloth only to recall how more than fifty years ago the family assembled to break bread together in celebration of what was believed to be Great Grandfather Wilson's 106th birthday in Detroit.

Let Us Break Bread Together

Let us break bread together on our knees.
Let us break bread together on our knees.
When I fall on my knees
With my face to the rising sun;
Oh, Lord, have mercy on me.

A Negro Spiritual

My Stevenson Great Grandparents had established the tradition of gathering for elaborate family reunions at their sprawling Georgia homestead prior to the turn of the twentieth century. So now years later Great Grandfather Wilson's birthday had come to mean family gatherings in the North. There, my Great Grandfather Wilson administered to the children a surefire word from a healing tree.

After the Great War—WW Two that is—kinfolk gathered from the four corners of the earth to celebrate life, once more. It was in the company of bubbly daughter Mary and husband and cool Joe McClendon, the patriarch Wilson, dressed in a starched white shirt, his broad shoulders peaking through a trim, charcoal three-piece suit, loosely fitted tie wrapped around his neck, made the trek to Motor City. My Great Grandfather Wilson

Stevenson gave the appearance of a man perhaps thirty years his junior. Graced with a hearty smattering of youthful good looks, a receding cotton hairline was the only telltale of approaching advanced age; as best as he recollected on his upcoming birthday he was going to be 106.

Wilson counted it all a blessing—to have fought in the Civil War and lived through two great wars. That day in Detroit, the centenarian Wilson counted off 225 people there at the birthday celebration. Why, he reckoned there was mo' kinfolk in the party than all the folks living back in Salt Springs, Georgia. There, he counted several children, 21 grandchildren, 28 great-grandchildren, 5 great-great-grandchildren, and 154 nieces and nephews.

Now that was a heap of kinfolk for anyone to behold and they was all gathered with one purpose—to celebrate Wilson 'Dad' Stevenson's long life. What a legacy that was! Well, that made his heart full too. Down his weathered cheeks tears came streaming. As earlier mentioned, his birthday, most importantly now, meant family gatherings and that year's birthday celebration in Motor City especially was special with the War coming to a close and all.

Freedmen's Invocation

Great Grandfather Wilson cried now more in freedom than ever he ever did in bondage. In the evening the Stevenson family was gathering to break the bread of life. Before its close the patriarch drew them closer together for the invocation.

"Be nice to people wherever you go, because you need to keep in mind we've got people just about everywhere," My Stevenson Great Grandfather said. "Just don't know who might be some of our kinfolk!"

Made all the children, grandchildren, and great-grandchildren, great-great-grandchildren, and nieces and nephews wonder just who were their kinfolk anyway. For his parting benediction has been carried around the world, setting those once in bonds free, invoking liberty and loosing a healing spirit. Now Great Grandfather Wilson was always dispensing wisdom in some form or another.

Made You Wonder?

My Stevenson Great Grandfather left just about everybody scratching their head, wondering just who were our kinfolk. Now that freedmen Wilson sure dished out some food for thought. His wisdom has become precious keepsakes.

Oh, there's been a heap of blood, culture, and wisdom transferred! Child, come on now—can I get a witness!

You ever travel somewhere and meet folks that favored you or another family member. Well, made you wonder just a little. Didn't it? Made you scratch your head, too? Umh… "And so, just who is your people?"

Centenarian Wilson Stevenson's
Twelve Steps for a Long and Prosperous Life

1. Serve God and community, make time for a spiritual retreat;

2. Love family, attend a family reunion;

3. Pick your friends carefully;

4. Be nice to people wherever you go;

5. Watch your tongue, don't be judgmental, and mind your own business and leave other folks alone. Speak life to situations.

6. Walk and don't smoke nor drink liquor;

7. Eat smaller meals and keep your bowels open;

8. Work hard, don't complain, and take a risk;

9. Save, let your savings be your insurance, cut unnecessary costs;

10. Set higher goals and ignore the critics;

11. Stay abreast of the news and happenings, take a cultural excursion;

12. Take time to enjoy life, meditate on God's creation, and travel and see some of the great, big, old world.

Chapter Two
Wilson's Ashes

middle passage

they brought us over here
and we danced
and they said
they got rhythm.
they brought us over here
and we ran
and they said
take us to the championship.
they brought us over here
and we sang
and the angels in
heaven cried.

(for Ambrosia Shepherd)

In some circles the masks of slavery have not been removed. Through the art of shucking and jiving they shielded themselves with a finesse that became a hallmark of Black culture. Black males realized that they had been assigned an underdog role and learned to play the part. Enslaved Africans became adept at artfully reading the nonverbal cues of whites. During slavery masking was an effective mechanism for protection.

Great Disaster

Eannes Zurara, 15th century Portuguese historian left us with heart-wrenching eyewitness accounts of violent separations of African families following arrival in Portugal. Communal expressions of great disaster ranged from guttural moaning and weeping that recalls the blues to again and again striking their own faces and with great force throwing their bodies to the ground. These actions reflected the customs of mourning at burials in their homeland.

At the same time mother's attempt to protect their children with their very own bodies met with powerful blows. African male resistance, which would be difficult to squelch several centuries later, was countered with brute strength. Similar distressful scenes likely were repeated, as enslaved Africans got off ships in seventeenth century Barbados and eighteenth century British America colonies. Upset in the communal lives of other ethnic groups followed.

Gustavus Vassa a late eighteenth century African, was born in Benin, kidnapped, and sold, in America. He had no time to say goodbye to his family. He firmly took to task the United States for its system of racial slavery. He strongly disapproved of the separation of enslaved Africans and their families, which happened for economic reasons. An African view of dating with strict rules and values about sex and unthinkables about marriages to cousins likely was brought over the Atlantic Ocean. African communities centered upon extended family.

The African slave trade between the late 15th and mid 19th centuries began the Maafa, what is a Kiswahili word for the great disaster that led to the scattering of Africa's seed to the wind, the depopulating and underdevelopment of Africa, and development of a dehumanizing system of racial slavery in the Americas. Enslaved Africans were considered livestock and listed in farm journals along with mules, horses, and pigs. Slavery should be unacceptable in any form, though a milder version of slavery was practiced in African communities where slaves blended into society.

The Ashanti Empire of West Africa, for example, afforded slaves freedom to marry within the Ashanti community, testify in legal cases, own property. Such human rights were unheard of for enslaved Africans in the Americas.

First Africans

During the 1960s Malcolm X, twentieth-century black protest leader and author of *The Autobiography of Malcolm X* (1965), heightened the awareness of the black masses about the social stigma of slavery and racism. Malcolm X publicly lamented the tragic loss of indigenous African naming practices, moreover the stripping of African cultural identities, in slavery's aftermath. Representing more than the names of exploitive masters, enslaved African-Americans' surnames however, revealed points of common origin on plantations, hope of continuity, and family pride.

Prior to the 1960s the African-American masses unfortunately all together missed out on valuable discussion of slave status. The present-day call for reparations by blacks, viewed as a legal request for the United States government to make financial restitution to the descendants of enslaved Africans for loss wages and material gains suffered them, due to a loss of inheritance, and their descendants has roots in slavery.

Up until recent times, Charleston, South Carolina, like other trading centers, disassociated itself with a significant role in the slave trade. The reluctance perhaps was due in part to a twentieth-century perception of social responsibility coupled with fear of potential adverse economic repercussions. Charleston was a recognized slave trading center, where Omar Ibn Said, a Muslim from the Senegal Gambia region of West Africa and likely war captive, arrived in 1807.

Eight years later, Ajar, another captive from West Africa, arrived in Charleston. Ajar's man-child Tony, who was held by a slaveowner Allen Little, was recognized as the great-grandfather of Malcolm Little, also known as Malcolm X. Many enslaved Africans, who came through ports in Georgia and South Carolina's coastal region, faced the challenge in integrating two worldviews—one African and the other European—thus began the process of acculturation.

South Carolina became home to a large number of blacks. The black majority provided a safe place for African traditions to survive. By

1720 Africans had held a majority over whites for more than a decade. Due to Lorenzo Turner's pioneering *Africanisms in the Gullah Dialect* (1949), it is generally accepted the language spoken by the offspring of enslaved Africans in coastal South Carolina and Georgia was a blend of English and language patterns what might be heard in West Africa.

South Carolina rice planters sought out to import Africans with valuable farming skills from the Grain Coast, now known as Sierra Leone. In 1685 enslaved Africans, who held knowledge of rice production and basketmaking, showed English settlers how to grow rice in the low country.

African Presence

The first generation of Africans found it hard to start families in the Americas. First, few first generation Africans lived a long time. Their untimely deaths, due to long and hard work days, poor diets, and bad housing, nipped in the bud any hope of folks having families.

Africans were exposed to barbaric, harsh punishments which ranged from being locked into iron head muzzles to maiming and castration. Other roadblocks to starting families included different languages, men living in same sex barracks style housing, and a short supply of black females.

The change from an African-based worldview to an American typically occurred earlier in the Chesapeake region than in the deeper South. The greater numbers of African children to those of Europeans in a region the increased likelihood the retention of African cultural practices survived. African traditions survived in the United States, as visible in the storytelling of the tar-baby and tortoise and hare folk tales along with spirituals. Dance, folk belief, and particular social norms were transported from Africa. African drums, banjo and xylophone-style instruments found there way in America. Diets, rich in rice, yams, okra, watermelon, peanuts and sorghum, resembled Africa.

Secret shipments of enslaved Africans continued to arrive as late as the 1850s off secluded coastal Georgia and South Carolina. The later in time the shipment of Africans was outlawed the increased likelihood African retentions persisted. Georgia and South Carolina however unofficially entertained the importation of Africans well into the nineteenth century.

In the United States the African slave trade was abolished by the federal government in 1808. The numbers remained relatively small but likely were concentrated in low country regions with high black concentrations. Conservative estimates placed the figures at a thousand annually over several decades. Six hundred thousand Africans had been brought to the United States, according to conservative estimates.

African Identity

Charles L. Blockson, author of the classic *Black Genealogy*, encourages that our children be nurtured in the appreciation of "their African identity and family history." With that thought in mind I wrote a family rap.

Black Family Rap

We are the children of those who would not die on the Middle Passage.
We are the children of those who trusted in God.
We are the children of those who received correction.
We are the children of those who would not accept "no" as an answer.
We are the children of those who would not bow to injustice.
We are the children of those who sought opportunity.
We are the children of those who loved themselves.
We are the children of those who remained vigilant.
We are the children of those who refused to give up hope.
We are the children of those who dared to dream.
We are the children of those who cared about one another.
We are the children of those who respected each other.
We are the children of those who answered the call to service.
We are the children of those who dared to be different.
We are the children!

Black males were marketable for their physical strength, which was highly prized in a labor demanding farming world. The number of black males topped females by almost two to one in some regions. Yet the black male remained the single greatest threat to white stability for his daring leadership and desire to revolt.

First generation African males tended to escape together in hopes of establishing a maroon colony. African society traditionally stressed communal living so enslaved Africans desperately sought a place to live together. When slave families later formed and faced separation, the male tended to be the one first sold on the block.

Separation was a slave's greatest fears. Auction records from New Orleans reflect that in the Deep South separation typically occurred. Children from age ten to twelve often were considered single and sold separately. Enslaved families responded to separation from running away to greater reliance upon extended family members, based on African traditions.

Others developed a look of indifference to conceal the hurt. Some slave mothers went into a depression. Scholars contend small free black slaveholders tended to purchase slave family members to protect them from separation and slavery.

The author poses with Pat Bearden, president of the International Sons and Daughters of Slave Ancestry, after giving his keynote address for the society's Juneteenth Celebration, DuSable Museum, Chicago, Illinois.

Wilson's Ashes

I wrote and performed the one-man satire, Wilson's Ashes as the keynote speaker for the International Sons and Daughters of Slave Ancestry's First Juneteenth, held at the DuSable Museum, Chicago on June 28, 1998. Through the art of shucking and jiving enslaved Africans shielded themselves with a finesse that became a hallmark of Black culture.

As the family story sheds light, African Americans have inherited from their ancestors a complex system of masking what they think and feel to protect themselves from emotional anguish and even physical abuse.[1] Nearly 40,000 African Americans served in the Confederate ranks, often slaves were assigned to masters as bodyservants.[2]

Our Harps Hang On The Willows

Clipped-winged cherubim.
Like nomads wander the earth;
Reapers of gold, some gatherers,
Others sowers, soulful eyes athirst.

Kaffir boy, driven to plow fields,
Chants: "Steve Biko, he is our own,"
Born into their pride, lion's mane
Chieftains wear,
Scarification marks the tribe.

The spring of 1849 there were several big frosts which was quite strange for that time of the year. The normally lush countryside looked blighted like in the fall. An old negro conjurer woman, who closely watched the spirit world, looked upon the unnatural weather with foreboding. When the sudden death of Marse Moore Stevenson followed, ripping the slave world apart, she tied the unnatural weather to a bad omen. Poor fellow left a widow, Missus Linnah, and eight, hungry children.[3]

The quarters had not been shaken like this since the vilest man on the earth, Prosper Johnson come through these parts. He tote a purse full from the sale of thirty negroes.[4] He cut a road headed due west through the Alabamie frontier.

Now, Marse Moore was missed 'round de quarters. Poppa Archie Willie and him settled the wild Creek frontier and they got pretty tight, dislodging rattlesnake dens, clearing farmland and fighting wild injuns. He and Poppa Archie Willie was there together when they buried the first white person—his name was Pollard. They laid that Pollard boy to rest—he was but a little biddy fellow—by a large poplar tree.

Not far from there he shot at a panther, stalking Archie Willie.[5] Those was some tough times. Colored and whites had better watched each other's back. Else they'd be found dead together.

Of hearty Scotch Irish Presbyterian stock rock 'em, sock 'em through-and-through, Marse Moore he was no pansy. Our white Stevensons was tough, thrifty, hardworking, what some folks called scrappers. So it came sort of natural—gettin' in thar and kickin' some butt. Settlin' wild frontiers and the like, guess, adventure had to be in our blood.

Now dem Stevensons, was good to their colored people, about as good as you find in dem slavery days. And they was just about as fine a class of white folks, as you'd ever want to meet. Why Marse Moore told Poppa Archie Willie that he was worth his weight in gold!

Why we was livin' and knew it! Oh yes we was! We had our own water-powered grist mill and three cotton gins. There was a fine big house. Thought we was somebody! We had somethin' to point to.

Long after freedom came Poppa Archie Willie still was heard calling Marse Moore, an aristocrat. Marse Moore was a judge.[6] Thar was a long line of dem, goin' all the way back to the Revolutionary War and Belfast, Ireland.[7] Heard tell, we owned the courthouse grounds. Now, our Stevensons was what you might call big shots back in the day. Other niggaras on other plantations couldn't tell our folks nothin'.

Oh, but how the mighty fell! The next generation of Stevensons was not as aristocratic. Marse Moore's absence called for them to step forward. Now they was good people, but they was just more like common folks, just trying to make a living, having bills and that. You see, young Massas Joseph and Augustus and little Missy Emily was fixin' to attend school, the Newnan Academy they was in the fall of the year.[8]

Reckon, that's why they did what dey did. Commenced, rounding up the colored and they's chillen, dividing them twenty-seven or so up and before long fixing prices to dem. That's how we and our little white playmates came to be invested with slavery's mantle. Nine bunches were counted off real proper-like, three to a bunch, before throwing numbers in a hat.

Colored kinfolk was highly valued and important, so we figured. Why Ma Hattie conceived more than fourteen chillen and spent eleven years with her belly full and she fetched a good price, almost as much as a good, healthy man.[9] Each suckling she dropped put 'bout two hundred dollars in the Stevenson's pouch.

Lord knows, didn't want no squabbling among the poor white chillen. That's how Marse Moore would have wanted it.

Now, the slaveowning Stevensons divvied up our side of the family. We was divvied up right with Henry the bay mule, Fox the midnight mule, and the hogs and the chickens.[10]

Sure the womenfolk and children carried on. Made quite a racket! What you think? Still, the menfolk sucked the pain in, holdin' it close to them like. They kept a stiff upper lip through it all but was hurting inside.

Missus Linnah, God bless her soul, she showed us a wonderful kindness! She tried to keep us chillen under twelve with our parents. Showed us a kindness. She done that so Poppa, Ma and us little biddies was all able to live together. So you see how much she thought about our folks!

Poor Missus was, just like the rest of white women in dem times, not in power. Before all was said and done the old poor widow lady was in debt. Commenced selling Poppa. He went to Major Brewster and was left seeing Ma and us chillen when he could.

As fall turned to winter, followed by spring, the cycle of life repeating itself, Wilson, folks 'round the quarters called him Wils, sprouted into a young fellow. He was a fine looking man. Hee! Hee!—sort of favored me. His selection as a stud was to be expected, it came as no surprise to us.

Still got some of them hiring out receipts. Hired out was just white folks' fancy way of saying rented. You see, it says right here back in 1858 a twenty-something Wils was hired to L. Leply for $80.00. That's how in he helped and paid for that white Stevenson gal's learning.[11]

Ole massa say, "Wench get in thar."

Wils, he be in thar waitin', and sometimes could hear her heart poundin' away. Wils say that work wasn't everything it was cut out to be—spread his seed far and wide.

Wils lived to keep his good white folks in stitches. Reckon, that led to his selection as Confederate bodyservant over others. Missy Emily married Marse George Fambrough, whom he followed into conflict.[12]

"I could piss straight up in the air and run under it before it hits the ground," Wils boasted about his military service.

Before the conflict few slaves had ventured beyond the Gate City. In the quarters the colored Stevenson boy was the object of envy.

Now the Stevenson boys wasn't that all up on national politics, but then who was? All the boys truly knew for certain was that it was in their best interest to look out for their kinfolk and Georgia home. Other issues got somewhat muddled. The boys wanted freedom, but then there was no guarantee that it was coming from the North.

Dem boys relied upon their mother wit as best as they could and fig-ured the whole thing out: If the 'federates won, they'd free them out of gratitude. If the Yankees won, they'd punish the rebby boys and free all the colored out of spite. Anyhow that's how dey looked at it. And there was no use frettin' 'bout matters—It was all in the good Lord's hands.

Dem devilish Yankees torching what we done worked so hard to build. Dat Sherman was a mess! You see, those 'federates near licked dem Yankees. There were jus' too many of dem in blue.[13]

The Stevenson boys shone as valiant heroes for a glorious moment, but as it were. The boys was all around soldiers, not only striking camp but digging trenches and foraging.[14]

Whatever the colored Yankees was doing for the blues the Stevenson boys was proud to do for they's side. Wils and brother, Dennis, dawned the butternut and protected their masters from Union gunfire by firing at the enemy. Both colored Confederate and Union troops alike faced a segregated world and hoped to prove themselves to the world-at-large.

There was heaps of Colored 'federates from Gettysburg to Ole Miss. Now, Confederate Mary was the gray's secret weapon. She were a colored spy. She were the 'federate version of Harriet Tubman and wreaked havoc behind them union lines.

Dem Colored Stevenson boys witnessed some harrowing times. It was tough keeping dey's eyes peeled for ole massa. Lord knows they tried dey bes' to keep dem out of harm's way. Now Major T.F. Jones, took a hit right smack in the groin. Whew, that thang smarted! Had de Major laid up for awhile.

Wils done the right thing watching over Marse George, like he did, things being the way they was. Another kind of man might have skipped out after the going got rough: Ole massa got captured, leaving dem high and dry, but not Wils.

Wils always said: Marse George had his own family to look out for, and I mine.

During slavery masking was an effective mechanism for protection. In southern lore there was no more celebrated figure than the 'federate body servant. At Fort Mill, South Carolina today there stands a monument recognizing them: Dedicated to the faithful slaves who, loyal to a sacred trust toiled for the support of the Army with matchless devotion and with sterling fidelity guarded Our Confederate States of America.

Colored hands tended to cavalrymen' steeds, erected fortifications and constructed railways. Some worked with explosives and armament production. Others were grand musicians, playing triumphant battle charges. Military service was a great equalizer that made the playing field level for all.

Across the country I have performed the one-man act, based on my meticulous genealogical research as portrayed through the vivid narrative of a slave ancestor Wilson Stevenson (1838-1948), who in 1948 was the last known person to be born in slavery and serve in the Confederacy living in Pennsylvania.

Life Applications

1. What is the significance of the word Maafa?

2. According to Alexis de Tocqueville (a Frenchman), author of *American Institutions and Their Influence* (New York, Barnes, 1851), "the Negro makes a thousand fruitless efforts to insinuate himself upon men who repulse him; he conforms to the taste of his oppressors, adopts their opinions, and hopes imitating them, to form a part of their community. Having been told from infancy, that his race is naturally inferior to that of the Whites, he asserts to the proposition and is ashamed of his own nature. In each of h*is* features he discovers a trace of slavery, and if it were in his power, he would willingly rid himself of everything that makes him what he is." Discuss this statement in light of *Wilson's Ashes*.

3. Compare and contrast Wilson Stevenson's service in the Confederate ranks and his colored Union counterparts.

Endnotes

1   Richard Majors and Janet Mancini Bilson, *Cool Pose: The Dilemmas of Black Manhood in America* (New York: Simon and Schuster, 1992), pp. 59-65.

2   "What the Confederacy Stood For," *Opportunity Journal, Equal Opportunity Journal* (February 1998), p. 55.

3   Mary G. Jones and Lily Reynolds, Coweta County Chronicles (Easley, South Carolina: Southern Historical Press, 1928), p. 95.

4   Mary G. Jones and Lily Reynolds, *Coweta County Chronicles* (Easley, South Carolina: Southern Historical Press, 1928), p. 95.

5   Ibid., pp. 493-4.

6   Files of Georgia Department of Archives and History.

7   Jessie McDaniel Hamrick, "The Stephensons of Carroll County: A History of a Family," *The Carroll County* (Georgia) *Genealogical Quarterly* 1:2 (August 1980), p. 40.

8   In 1850 the Newnan Academy issued its first catalogue. The student list was published in the 31 December 1926 *Newnan Herald.*

9   Figured out her value the same way as a man's, by multiplying the price of cotton per pound by 10,000, she being worth it, pound for pound. Sarah Blackwell Gober Temple, *The First Hundred Years* (Atlanta: Cherokee Publishing, 1980), p. 203.

10 Moor Stephenson Estate Records. Inventory and Appraisement, 2 July 1849. Probate Court, Coweta County, Georgia; Sarah Blackwell Gober Temple, *The First Hundred Years* (Atlanta: Cherokee Publishing Company, 1980), p. 203.

11 Annual Returns. Book I. Probate Court, Coweta County, Georgia.

12 Minute Book D, p. 238. Ordinary Court, Coweta County, Georgia; Letters from James Doster to author, 7 Feb. 1982 and 2 March 1982; "Former slave, 100 today, to be honored by family," Sharon (PA) Herald, 3 Nov. 1938, p. 1.

13 List of Confederate Soldiers, Probate Court Coweta County, Georgia, pp. 62-5; "Ex-Slave Marks 103rd Birthday," *Sharon* (Pennsylvania) *Herald,* 3 November 1941, pp. 1, 6.

14 Richard Rollins, "Black Confederates at Gettysburg," Journal of Confederate History Series, 11 (1994), pp. 129-41; Leon F. Litwack, *Been In the Storm So Long* (New York: Random House, 1980), p. 37.

April 24, 1993 meeting of Mid-Atlantic Regional Council African-American Genealogical Groups at African-American Historical Society Museum, Jersey City, NJ.

Chapter Three
How To Begin

Across the country people have discovered what a rewarding experience tracing your roots can be. A generation, who got hold of the 1960's slogans of "Black is beautiful," hungered for more. As earlier mentioned, the phenomenal success of Alex Haley's popular television miniseries *Roots* spoke to a deep human need, to know who you are. Alex Haley's *Roots*, which traces his family story back to the furthest back ancestor Kunta Kente, aired to a large viewing audience in the 1970s. The family story was the topic of considerable conversation, as evidenced by an increase in African-American family and genealogical organizations across the United States.

Ten years later, author of *Somerset Homecoming* (1988) Dorothy Spruill Redford, now site director at the Somerset Place, organized a reunion of more than two thousand descendants of enslaved Africans and their captors. In more recent times Edward Ball's story of intertwined lives led by slaves and their masters *Slaves in the Family* (Ballantine Book 1999) received a National Book Award.

Who are my people? Genealogist Karim Aldridge Rand grew up wanting to know more about his identity. He lamented little material existed about the African-American experience in history books, in particular social studies textbooks in public school. How did I come to be here? "Who am I?" was the fundamental question that he was looking to answer. He had done some preliminary interviews and had reached the place where he was stumped. He had confronted a major obstacle that all researchers come to face, though organization surely has aided in his success.

He was a college student when he expressed an interest in tracing his roots to me. I took him to the National Archives and Records Administration, where I oriented him to the finding aids and gave an overview of the microfilm collection. I concluded the day's instruction with a final product—copy of a census record enumerating Rand's Aldridge ancestor.

Essentially, I was to develop a framework and action plan for him to conduct his research. He was ecstatic! Over the next four years he made the regular trek from Howard University to the National Archives, until his departure from the nation's capitol.

Preparation will be the key to success. Karim Aldridge Rand, like most of us, just needed some basic tools and guidelines to get underway. For those of you who do not own a personal computer or Mac, there are a few things that you can do. He, for example, set up a binder system for each family line. He used a binder and tabs labeled with research subjects. Sample subject headings might include "Oral History," "1930 Census Records," "Bible Records," and "Marriage Licenses."

You might consider a fireproof file cabinet or a box in a bank vault for priceless items. If you own a computer and are a beginning genealogist, you might look into software and an Internet Service Provider that offers high speed connectivity at a reasonable cost. Family Tree Maker is a good software package. The biggest challenge of tracing your roots has got to be getting prepared for what will promise to be an odyssey.

Family Relationships

CHART NUMBER _____

GENERATION I _____
            (yourself)

1 _____ Yourself _____
(yourself)   year of birth/place   year of death/place

GENERATION II — PARENTS

2 _____ Your Father _____
Father of #1   year of birth/place   year of death/place

3 _____ Your Mother _____
Mother of #1   year of birth/place   year of death/place

GENERATION III — GRANDPARENTS

4 _____ Your Paternal Grandfather _____
Father of #2   year of birth/place   year of death/place

5 _____ Your Paternal Grandmother _____
Mother of #2   year of birth/place   year of death/place

6 _____ Your Maternal Grandfather _____
Father of #3   year of birth/place   year of death/place

7 _____ Your Maternal Grandmother _____
Mother of #3   year of birth/place   year of death/place

GENERATION IV — GREAT-GRANDPARENTS

8 _____

Father of #4   year of birth/place   year of death/place

9 _____

Mother of #4   year of birth/place   year of death/place

10 _____

Father of #5   year of birth/place   year of death/place

11 _____

Mother of #5   year of birth/place   year of death/place

12 _____

Father of #6   year of birth/place   year of death/place

13 _____

Mother of #6   year of birth/place   year of death/place

14 _____

Father of #7   year of birth/place   year of death/place

15 _____

Mother of #7   year of birth/place   year of death/place

Figure 1 ANCESTOR TABLE

To trace your roots is to identify blood relatives. If you are trying to figure out two people are related, you might find benefit from a Relational Calculator www.aagsclev.org/toolsf.htm. Beware, in the African-American tradition there sometimes appear fictive kin, who were not blood relatives. Great-Uncle John, who might have had strong bonds to your family members, may not be a blood relative. Patterns of naming a child after an aunt, uncle, great-uncle, great-aunt, or grandparent existed as far back as slavery.

Family members, who have passed, that make up your direct line of descent, such as your great-grandparents and great-great-grandparents are known as ancestors. Use ancestor tables or ancestry charts, which are available at a genealogical store, to record your information for ancestors along with sources and dates. Ancestry charts list your ancestors' birth, marriage, and death dates and the places where each event occurred. A deceased brother or sister of an ancestor is referred to as a collateral ancestor.

A family chart is used to record information for a nuclear family or single parent household. Tony Burrough's *Black Roots: A Beginner's Guide to Tracing the African American Family Tree* (Fireside 2001) is an excellent resource on documentation and methodology for beginners to intermediate genealogical researchers.

Be aware of naming practices in your family. Unusual naming practices are keys to the past. Recently, I have learned that my Great-great Grandmother Delita Chatman was a Black Indian name. Family members hid our unusual names, including Etania and Rillis, were Native American.

Few enslaved Africans were fortunate enough to retain a version of their original African surnames, though the Quanders, who have a documented presence of more than 320 years in America, have this distinction. In 1984, the Quander United Incorporated, a non profit historical and research association, held a three day family celebration commemorating three hundred years in the Americas. Quander is a derivation of the Fanti surname "Kwandoh" or "Amkwandoh," which has name recognition in present-day Ghana to the Cape Coast.

The enslaved Africans passed on their name and pronunciation to future generations, though through time the original spelling was to become anglicized by British colonists. If you locate any unusual names in your family, Oganna Chuka-Oris's *Names from Africa* (Johnson Publishing 1972) is an excellent source. Roma Jones Stewart's *Africans in Georgia 1870* (Homeland Publications 1993) is a helpful source in locating names of African ancestors.

Following Emancipation African-Americans sometimes held two or more different surnames, which associated them with various past events. Some retained surnames of former plantations where they and their family lived together. Others who ran away changed their names to elude bounty hunters.

In slavery's closing the selection of a surname signified more than the name of a previously captor, but represented families of origin, prior places of residence, and family pride. Perhaps, there are first names that occur over and over in your family? I knew my cousin was named after our aunt. Still I pleasantly was surprised to discover in my research familiar sounding names, because the naming of my mother, aunts and uncles after their aunt, uncles, and grandparents followed what was a time honored practice in the African-American tradition.

CHART NUMBER _____

GENERATION I _____ Roland Barksdale-Hall _____
　　　　　　　　(yourself)

1 _____ Roland Barksdale-Hall _____ Sharon, PA _____
(yourself)　　　　year of birth/place　　　　year of death/place

GENERATION II — PARENTS

2 _____ Clarence Hall (Barksdale) 1926 Eufala, AL _____ 1979 Youngstown, OH
Father of #1　　　　year of birth/place　　　　year of death/place

3 _____ Anna Steverson 1918 Paulding County, GA 1982 Farrell, PA _____
Mother of #1　　　　year of birth/place　　　　year of death/place

GENERATION III — GRANDPARENTS

4 _____ Jessie Hall 1901 ___ 1980 Haines City, FL _____
Father of #2　　　　year of birth/place　　　　year of death/place

5 _____ Camilla Barksdale (Browder) _____ Tuscaloosa, AL
Mother of #2　　　　year of birth/place　　　　year of death/place

6 _____ Etania Steverson 1871 Newnan, GA 1943 Wheatland, PA
Father of #3　　　　year of birth/place　　　　year of death/place

7 _____ Your Maternal Grandmother _____
Mother of #3　　　　year of birth/place　　　　year of death/place

GENERATION IV — GREAT-GRANDPARENTS

8 _____ ? _____
Father of #4　　　　year of birth/place　　　　year of death/place

9 _____?_____

Mother of #4   year of birth/place   year of death/place

10 _____ Charles Barksdale Midway, AL _____

Father of #5   year of birth/place   year of death/place

11 _____ Cassie Massey Clio, AL _____

Mother of #5   year of birth/place   year of death/place

12 ___ Wilson Stevenson 1838 Newnan, GA 1948 West Middlesex, PA ___

Father of #6   year of birth/place   year of death/place

13 _____ Rillis Chatman 1847 _ 1917 Lithia Springs, GA ____

Mother of #6   year of birth/place   year of death/place

14 ____ Grant Fielder 1868 Clayton County, GA 1944 Douglasville, GA _

Father of #7   year of birth/place   year of death/place

15 _____ Anna Lindly 1871 Mableton, GA 1950 Douglasville, GA __

Mother of #7   year of birth/place   year of death/place

Figure 2 COMPLETED ANCESTOR TABLE

Telling Our Stories

Genealogist Robert H. Williams urges that you take time out to write your life story. "Many genealogists are so busy researching deceased kin that they forget to do their autobiography. At any rate, do your autobiography (or have some one else do it for you). Distribute it to relatives as well."

You are telling your life story for future generations, who will be so glad that you took the time to share a gift from the heart. Your story can take a thematic format or progress from present to past. To jot down what you know about your family, folklore, and community will get you started on your life story.

What was your favorite pastime growing up? How did you spend holidays? What is your name? Do you have a nickname? How did you come by the name? When and where were you born? Who were your parents? Who were your brothers or sisters? Where did you attend school? What was your first job? If you are married, how was the courtship? When were you married and to whom? Where did you and your spouse first live? What are the names of your children? When and where were they born? Any memorable circumstances related to their birth and development? Who were your grandparents? What were their occupations? Where did they live? Where were they buried? Do the same for your great-grandparents?

Answers to questions like who, where, when and sometimes if available why and how will be considered treasures. Reveal a little something about who you are. Just be sure to let your family know what made you tick.

Life Timeline
- ▼ Birth
- ▼ Baptism
- ▼ School Begins
- ▼ Social Security Card
- ▼ Driver's License
- ▼ High School Graduation
- ▼ Military
- ▼ College
- ▼ Job
- ▼ Marriage
- ▼ Birth of Children
- ▼ Retirement

Sample Autobiographical Sketch

Ollie Valera Matilda Stoney was born June 9, 1885 in Warren, Pennsylvania, the daughter of Joseph and Emma Stoney. In later years, the family moved to Stoneboro, Pennsylvania. My father, Joseph Stoney, was a chef at the Lake House Hotel...; my mother was a seamstress.

Ollie attended 1st, 2nd, and 3rd grades of school in Stoneboro. Her mother became ill in November, 1893, and died in May, 1894, she was ill for six months. She was buried at the White Chapel Cemetery at Leesburg, Pennsylvania.

Four children were born to Joseph and Emma Stoney: George (died in infancy), Joseph Edward, Ollie, and Elizabeth. The children were raised by their mother's parents, George and Caroline Richards Lewis at Indian Run, Mercer County, Pennsylvania.

In September, 1894, Ollie went to school in a one room school—a large, red brick building. Her first teacher was Mr. Bowman. He taught all children from the 1st to the 8th grades (the complete teacher they were called at the time)...

Our home in Stoneboro was a two-story, five room white house with a front and back porches, a gift from my mother's parents, George and Caroline Lewis... My grandparent's home was a white bungalow with six rooms and attic, front porch, and four large maple trees in the yard. The parlor (living room) was a great novelty to me, with Brussels carpet, a square iron black stove with nickel trim and coal bucket to match, a five-piece set of heavy plush furniture—two divans (soldier blue and dark red), red rocking chair, two armless chairs (old rose and green) and marble top stands...

Grandmother was an excellent cook. I was taught to cook, bake, and mend. It is a busy life to live on a farm, early to bed and early to rise... Grandpa raised all the food that we used. We had six cows, a team of horses, and chickens. We sold eggs at 10 cents per dozen, butter at 12 cents per pound, and live chickens at 25 cents... Grandpa was very deaf, he lost his hearing in the Civil War 1861... When it was time for dinner, he could not hear the dinner bell (all farmers had dinner bells), so I would go up to the field and get him...

My winter sport was ice skating. Thanksgiving, Christmas, and the New Year was great happiness for us. As Grandpa always bought a large, live goose (from our neighbor) for Thanksgiving dinner... Our grandparents were wonderful in so many ways. Santa Claus came to see us for Christmas and New Year's with gifts of apparel, candy, and some toys...

My great-grandparents (my mother's grandparents)—Pap Richards was a slave. He married a white woman from Pittsburgh, Pennsylvania, her name was Mary Elizabeth... She gave him twelve children.

Genealogical Society Checklist

▼ Offers research assistance in preparing queries and search strategies;

▼ Holds workshops, seminars, and conferences where opportunities to answer questions exist;

▼ Undertakes indexing African-American newspapers, slave records, transcribing cemetery records, collecting funeral home programs;

▼ Publishes newsletter, journal or books;

▼ Hosts an up to date Website and/or research database;

▼ Sponsors tours and research trips, newspaper column, regional meetings;

▼ Organizes state interest clubs;

▼ Maintains surname directories, ancestry charts and library;

▼ Participates in the Federation of Genealogical Societies;

▼ Recognizes achievement in African American genealogy and history;

▼ Promotes cultural awareness.

Genealogical Societies

To join a genealogical society is a must do. Genealogist Robert H. Williams says, "There you will be able to network with others. It came in handy for me, as I met someone on my paternal side that was of great help to me. She was from the same area as my paternal grandfather was, and was able to help me fill in much of the slave history on his side. You never know what is in store for you."

The Afro-American Historical and Genealogical Society (AAHGS), has chapters and affiliates throughout the United States (see Appendix A for genealogical society listing). I have a longstanding relationship with AAHGS. I am an AAHGS life member, founder of the AAHGS

Pittsburgh, and former book review editor for the scholarly *Journal of the Afro-American Historical and Genealogical Society.* AAHGS publishes a bi-monthly newsletter. Barbara D. Walker's *Index to the Afro-American Historical and Genealogical Society Quarterly Issues of 1980-1990* is a valuable resource. The AAHGS annual conference, held during October, encourages scholarly research in Black history and genealogy.

Check with the genealogical society about the availability of ancestry charts, family charts, and census forms for accurate record keeping. The benefits include quality programming, networking, and good fellowship. Pick a genealogical society with programming and services tailored to your interests.

Thursday, February 4, 1982—*The Newnan Times-Herald*—7B

Treetops To Roots

By Mrs. R. T. [Norma] Gunby, Sr.
Newnan-Coweta Historical Society

A good turnout for the January meeting. Vinnie Rosenzweig presented the program on local Craftsman Architecture. Slides were shown representing different things and many of the local homes were shown in this presentation.

The new officers took over for the year and many rejoined for the year at this first meeting.

Coweta County Genealogical Society

This Thursday (February 4) is the first Thursday in the month and this means that it is time for the Board of Directors meeting. Be sure to get any ideas or suggestions to one of them before the meeting.

Georgia Research Workshop

The Augusta Genealogical Society and Augusta College Department of Continuing Education are co-sponsoring this interesting workshop. It will be held February 20th at the Augusta College Activities Center in Augusta. It will be lead by Kenneth H. Thomas, Jr. (Genealogical columnist for the Sunday Atlanta Journal-Constitution).

If any of you have relatives in Augusta, this would be a good time to visit them.

Other Articles

Did you like the Mortality Schedule as an article? Would you like others? Would you like to have a listing of the 1827 Land Lottery of Coweta county? There are over 300 land lots and this would have to be distributed over a period of weeks. What would help you the most? Write and send me some items that you would like to see in this column.

Query

I am a senior at the University of Pittsburgh — I am doing a research project on my family tree — I have traced one line of my family tree back to Newnan, Georgia in the 1830's.

I am searching for any information available on a George Fambrow. He fought for the Confederate side in Georgia during the Civil War. My maternal great-grandfather, Wilson Steverson, was a slave of George Fambrow. I often found the Steverson name misspelled Stevenson. Wilson was born in Newnan November 3, 1858 to slaves Archie and Harriet. He was one of 14 children. Wilson fought alongside his master during the Civil War. After being freed he emigrated from Coweta county.

In 1938, Wilson's brother, Dennis Steverson was still living in Newnan at the age of 98. (I have gotten in touch with two of Dennis' grandchildren and they will write you).

Roland C. Hall, 939 Baldwin Avenue, Sharon, Pa. 16146.

1850 Georgia Mortality Census Schedule for Coweta County

Name	Age	Sex	State Born	Mo. of Death	Mar/ Wid.
Bates, David	30	m	Ga.	Jan.	M
Newman, C.	9	m	Ga.	Oct.	
Arnold, Martha E.	24	f	Ga.	March	M
Arnold, Lelia	5/12	f	Ga.	April	
Maddox, Susan	25	f	Ga.	Feb.	W
Kelly, Moses	53	m	S.C.	Jan.	M
Skinner, Martha	13	f	Ga.	Sept.	
Bell, Martha A.	26	f	Ga.	Aug.	M
Brown, Amos T.	5/12	m	Ga.	Dec.	
Thompson, Ann	85	f	Ga.	March	W
Pittard, Eliza M.	5	f	Ga.	Jan.	
Smith, Sara E.	1	f	Ga.	Sept.	
Maddox, Elizabeth	77	f	Ga.	Feb.	W
Waldrop, R. W.	38	m	S.C.	Jan.	M

The author mans the Black Genealogy booth at the National Council of Negro Women Black Family Reunion, National Mall, Washington, D.C.

Donna Beasley, along with Roland Barksdale-Hall, who shared his intriguing family stories in Beasley's book, at program sponsored by African-American Genealogical Society of Cleveland, Ohio.

Networking

Information which comes to you through networking should always be listed according to the source and verified through documentation. Beware of advertisements of books that claim to trace your family. One individual purchased a book reporting to be their family history for $50.00, assuming it was a book written by a family member. There was deep disappointment in receiving a generic heraldry book along with a list of names generated from national telephone directories. So there remains plenty of work undone tracing your roots.

Checklist of Things To Look for Around the House

▼ Family Bibles
▼ Photographs
▼ Correspondence
▼ Funeral home programs
▼ Membership Dues Cards
▼ Insurance Policies
▼ Insignia on cups, jewelry, pens or clothing
▼ Membership Dues Cards

Family Bibles

Family Bibles can be treasure troves of priceless information. I have found from a child's lock of hair to certificates in their leaves. I almost missed out on a gem because an elder did not realize that my repeated references to family documents included the family Bible. It so happened that another elder down the road apiece told me to go back there and fetch the family Bible. The oldest family Bible on record turned out to be my Great-great grandmother's Bible, which was found nestled in a weathered captain's trunk of a fourth generation descendant.

What a thrill it was to hold something in my hand that connected me to my enslaved ancestors! The tattered heirloom's faded leaves with script, barely discernible, showed wear from use, the binding and title page having been long gone. I took a deep breathe before looking inside. "Margaret Lindley wife of John Lindley left or departed this life February 11, 1885." An earlier entry of a birth supported what census takers had reported that Great-great Grandmother remained weak after the last birth of her child.

Photographs

The search in the attic revealed an old family photograph. I was only able to identify three individuals in the photograph, but it is important to make every possible effort to identify those in photos. Later in my research I found relatives in Georgia who were able to name all the individuals in that photo. I located a brief biographical sketch on the photographer in Herman Mason, Jr.'s *Going Against the Wind: A Pictorial History of African-Americans in Atlanta*. I was able to use clothing styles, the buggies in the background, and the photographer's name to arrive with an approximate date.

Sometimes other photos were placed behind one another for safe keeping in frames. Carefully look to see if there were names, places, and dates scribbled on the back of old photos. Ask if you might be able to scan or copy the photo. You can make a negative and store in a fireproof box or vault. Assure the relative you will return the picture undamaged. In the long run it will be worth the cost and effort. For more information about the care of photographs check at your library.

Genealogist Robert H. Williams stresses. "Some of the photos in your collection may actually be originals. One should try and have a negative made of each of your original photos."

Funeral Home Programs

The funeral home program is a distinctive African-American tradition. Elaborate, if not ornate, celebrations of family members' Homegoing Services are rooted in a rich African-centered tradition. Hard to find, if not impossible, answers to how and sometimes why family made certain choices about migration can be found, as revealed in the following from my cousin's:

> *Recognizing the limited opportunities for minorities in the South, Charles Barksdale chose to move to Detroit, Michigan in 1945. He opened his heart and doors of his home for many. He was instrumental in helping other young blacks find work and settle in and around the Detroit area. In 1978… Charles retired and moved with his family back to Eufala. He rejoined the church of his youth St. Emmanuel A.ME.*

Funeral home programs are collected by the AAHGS Patricia Liddell Researchers and stored at the Carter G. Woodson Library, Chicago, Illinois.

Correspondence

Family members typically sent letters and postcards. Record the findings precisely as they appear.

> *Douglasville, Ga=12=5=1957*
>
> *I am sinding for my birth sirstockett my name is mamie fielder Stephenson my Husban name was Joe Stephenson*
>
> *My father name Grant fielder*
>
> *My mother name was anna linley*
>
> *I was born in Mableton Ga Cobb County Ga*
>
> *Mamie Stephenson*
>
> *Cincus Beauro*
>
> *Washington, D.C.*

Notice how I carefully recorded the script from an old letter that my Grandmother had written to the U.S. Census Bureau. The letter likely was written to verify her eligibility for retirement. I found the letter tucked away in her parent's Bible. Keep old letters and papers in an acid free folder. Proper record keeping in the beginning will prevent some problems later in the game. Keep accurate record of the source from which information came and the date of your research. Record postmark information to keep a record of when and from where mail originated.

Fraternal Group Records

Was a family member an Alpha, AKA, Kappa or Delta? Have other family members pledged the same sorority or fraternity? Family members' involvement in secret fraternal organizations, which allotted a valuable opportunity for both males and females to develop critical leadership skills, is well worth checking out. The goal should be more to understand what affiliations family members chose rather than to pry into the operations of members-only organizations, as their participation in these groups signaled progress toward the black middle class.

For more information on this topic, you might read William Alan Muraskin's *Black Mason: The Role of Fraternal Orders in the Creation of a Middle-Class Black Community* and Loretta J. Williams' *Black Freemasonry and Middle Class Realities*.

Fraternal group records hold genealogical treasures. Be aware that family patterns tend to emerge. According to *The History of Deborah Chapter Order of Eastern Star, Order of Eastern Star, Prince Hall Affiliation, Commonwealth of Pennsylvania, 1908-1981*, Sara Dillard Austin served in the highest rank in the Pennsylvania Order of

Eastern Star from 1973 to 1975. Her parents' involvement reflected similar interest. Elizabeth Dillard was a life member of the Order of Eastern Star, Daughter of Isis, and Court of Calanthe.

Thomas Henry Dillard became a charter member of his local Masonic lodge in 1916. He was a member of the Consistory, a life member of the Shriners, life member and patron of the Order of Eastern Star, and member of the Royal Arch. During the 1920s it was more common to find an African-American man belonging to Masonry, Odd Fellows, and Knights of Pythias (or Elks) than just Masonry and one of the others. My Uncle Samuel Malloy was a member of the Knights of Pythias, Masons, and Elks, while my Aunt Dorothy Malloy (my mother's sister) belonged to the female auxiliary of the Masons and Elks.

Look for clues of membership, such as membership cards, insignia on pens, jewelry, aprons, clothing, and paddles around the house, as well as grave markers at cemeteries. Proceed to check with local chapters or affiliates for photographs, induction dates, membership activity, and resolutions upon death.

Check to see if any of your family held insurance policies through fraternal groups, there may be records of pay outs as the endowment of the Knights of Pythias and its female auxiliary provided substantial death benefits. Bessie Matthews' financial card book of the Order of Calanthe, 1927-1929, showed a record of dues, taxes, and payments on endowment. The African American Knights of Pythias, considered the richest fraternal group with valuable real estate holdings, offered a lucrative endowment for its members during the early twentieth century.

Checklist of Public Records to Look for Outside the House

▼ Directories
▼ Newspapers
▼ Biographies
▼ Obituaries
▼ Libraries and Archives
▼ County Historical Societies

Directories

Directories will help in pinpointing arrivals and departures from locations. Many events I was told of occurred while family was living at a particular place. I knew where an event occurred, but the directory assisted in identifying when. Business districts and neighborhoods are listed sequentially block-by-block.

Older directories' listings included race, names of husband and wife and sometimes older children, employers, occupations, and status of property, if owned or rented. Using older directories, you can begin to reconstruct your ancestor's lives.

Newspapers

My hometown had news items in *The Pittsburgh Courier* and *The New York Age* during the early twentieth century. National editions of African-American newspapers like those along with *The Chicago Defender* had regional correspondents that provided coverage throughout the country. "Colored News" sections with highlights about travel, church and society were carried in majority presses.

James M. Rose's *Black Genesis: A Resource Book for African-American Genealogy* (Genealogical Publishing Company 2003) provides state-by-state listing of African-American newspapers, as many smaller African-American newspapers were discontinued.

Putting the Research Together: Case Study

Robert H Williams used various document sources in tracing his Banneker ancestry, much of which having already been cited in 1931 by George Simpson of Wilberforce University. Williams combined information gathered from Bible Records, Census, Vital Records, Cemetery Records along with courthouse records in Ohio, Virginia, and Maryland.

An Ohio cousin assisted in sharing research, which he verified. As earlier mentioned, it was through the LETT branch (his maternal line) that he found a connection to Banneker.

The missing documents if they ever existed are:

A. (My sixth great grandparents)—Molly Welsh and Bannka's marriage license. Our oral history says that Molly and Bannka were married. No dates were mentioned. Since miscegenation was unlawful in early Maryland, they may never have gotten a License. At least it has not been found.

(My fifth great grandparents)—Mary Banneky and Robert Banneky's marriage license, also not found. Likewise, our oral history says they were married. Being free people of color, they should have been in the records. It is believed that Mary and Robert got married in 1730 since their first child Benjamin Banneker was born on 9 November 1731.

B. (My forth great grandparents)—Jemima Banneker and Samuel Dulaney Lett's marriage document not found either. Again, our oral history said that Samuel Dulaney looked like a white man, and had Indian blood as well. His mother was a white woman. It may be because of his appearance that they were unable to get a license. Again, our oral history stated they were married. Thus far, I have been unable to verify this one way or the other.

The documents Robert H. Williams have are:

A. (My third great grandparents)—Aquilla Lett married Charity Cobbalor on September 1787 in the Evangelical Lutheran

Church in Frederick, Maryland. Charity was later known as Christina Cobbler

(My second great grandparents)—John Cummins married Susanna Lett on 25 November 1818 in Harrison County, Ohio.

(My first great grandparents)—Joseph Cummins married Esther Lett on 20 September 1860 in Berrien County, Michigan. A notation on the marriage record said: "NIGGERS.

(My grandparents)—William J. Hill married Almedia Cummings on 7 November 1887 in Mecosta County, Michigan. Her name was actually Merinda Ann Cummins. She changed her name, and was listed as White. William J. Hill was of Pennsylvania Dutch ancestry, German and French. Merinda Ann Cummins was mixed with Black, White and Red.

Biographies

Robert H. Williams made a point to read as much as he could about his Banneker connection. *The Dictionary of American Negro Biography*, edited by Rayford W. Logan and Michael R. Winston, published by W. W. Norton & Company, New York – London, copyright 1982, provided an excellent article on Banneker, the information being supplied by Mr. Silvio A. Bedini, a professor emeritus of the Smithsonian Institution in Washington, DC, who also wrote a more definitive biography *The Life and Times of Benjamin Banneker.*

Obituaries

To ensure that in the future more extensive local death records are available to African-American researchers at WRHS Society Library, the African-American Genealogical Society (AAGS) of Cleveland, Ohio, began indexing obituaries from the local black newspaper. The more supporting documents you have, enhances verification of past events.

If you know when an ancestor died, see if any of the local newspapers in your community has their obituary on file. An obituary provides relationships and a recap of an ancestor's life. Search for mortuary records. The possibility exists that some information that you gleaned may not be entirely accurate or incomplete. As earlier mentioned, always record the research findings precisely as you found them.

According to Charles L. Blockson, "Obituaries are very important. Some people save them. Whenever I read in the obituaries of people that I know or who have entered my life, I cut them out. Sometimes these obituaries are of distinguished people, oftentimes they're not. I put them on acid free paper and preserve them here in what is called a vertical file. Obituaries give good vital information."

Libraries

In America's heartland the Western Reserve Historical Society Library of Cleveland, Ohio, Allen County Public Library of Fort Wayne, Indiana, and Newberry Library of Chicago, Illinois are outstanding libraries with an emphasis upon genealogy.

As far back as 1867, the Western Reserve Historical Society (WRHS) was one of the first institutions in America to formally express interest in genealogy. Through the years, it's library sphere of interest has extended from New England to Georgia and west to the Mississippi River, however microfilm resources available at the library extend far beyond Cuyahoga County borders.

Although few institutions in the country have the complete United States federal population census schedule on microfilm, the decennial census, taken since 1790 is all available through 1930.

Valuable records at the WRHS Library include the following:
- ▼ Printed state census indexes through 1870,

- ▼ 1890 special census of Union veterans and their wives,

- ▼ Ohio mortality schedules listing deaths in 1850, 1860, and 1880,

- ▼ Cities directory for Cleveland,

▼ More than 3,000 manuscript Collections

▼ Union Catalog of American Genealogies,

▼ More than 60 microfilm rolls from the Ohio Surname Index to biographical material in various publication,

▼ More than 18,000 family histories.

WRHS research tools facilitate easy access to the library's numerous collections. Additionally researchers with a special interest in Cuyahogo County, Ohio, will find a treasure in the major African-American manuscript collections held by the Western Reserve Historical Society.

The African-American Archives focuses upon achievements going all the way back to Cleveland's founding in 1796. I was surprised to find a family member's name in Russell H. Davis' *Black Americans in Cleveland* published by the Associated Publishers in cooperation with the WRHS. I had not known that John Kellogg had been a city councilman.

With nearly sixty percent of its visitors registering as genealogists, the library's commitment to genealogy is steadily expanding. Fee-based library research services at over forty dollars per hour are available. As the recipient of the National Genealogical Society's Award of Merit for "being one of the finest genealogical libraries in the United States," the WRHS Library is prepared to assist.

The Library of Congress is the national library, located in Washington, D.C. It has copies of just about every book published. In addition the records of the National Association for the Advancement of Colored People, bound copies of *Flower of the Forest: Black Genealogical Journal* and much more are available there. Sandra Lawson's *Generations Past: A Selected List of Sources for Afro-American Genealogical Research* highlight specific research available at the Library of Congress.

Another valuable resource is the publication, *The African-American Mosaic*. Other notable libraries with special genealogical collections include the National Genealogical Society Library, Burton Historical Collection of the Detroit Public Library, Schomburg Collection of New York Public Library, and the Daughters of the American Revolution (DAR) Library.

County Historical Societies

I was disappointed to see in early county histories scant information about the African-American presence in both the North and South, though I have found maps and material about the culture and life helpful. I decided to make sure that under my watch our African-American stories were no longer to go untold. My beautiful people's stories just had to be told.

I still remember the glaring lack of my peoples' images in Mary J. Jones' *Coweta County Chronicles* (Southern Historical Press 1928) which provided coverage of the black belt. Sixty years later, The Newnan-Coweta Historical Society's *A History of Coweta County, Georgia*, was balm to a weary soul.

Family stories along with priceless vintage photos of the Wilson Stevenson family reunion, Howard Wallace Warner, African-American principal, and Lila P. Malcolm McGinty, who after her husband Andrew died, farmed, raised not only her children but her two deceased sister's six children, and left a "legacy of love, family, closeness, hard work, and desire for education" celebrated the lives of my people!

I was overjoyed in knowing the Mercer County Historical Society's 590-page book *Mercer County Pennsylvania Pictorial History 1800-2000* (Donning Company 2001) carried my people's story. What was gratifying that my people said that "their historian was to tell our story" and I was so honored to have appear several essays on the Black church, fraternal organizations and inventors. My people were no longer "invisible."

Life Application

1. What gift from the heart would you like to pass on to future generations?

2. Develop a research strategy for tracing your roots? What resources are required?

3. How might you ensure that the story of the African-American experience is told?

4. Reflect upon the testimony of Lila P. Malcolm McGinty, who after her husband Andrew died, farmed, raised not only her children but her two deceased sister's six children, and left a "legacy of love, family, closeness, hard work, and desire for education" How might you make a difference in the world?

Chapter Four
Art of Interviewing

Tapping our strong African-American oral tradition can make all the difference in the world. African-American families have been able to verify oral history, passed down from generation to generation. Minnie Shumate Woodson, a member of the Afro-American Historical and Genealogical Society, wrote a fictional work about the Hemings and Jefferson saga based on oral history and her extensive personal research.

Today, DNA testing further has leant support to what Thomas Woodson family members knew all along. Founding Father Thomas Jefferson and Sally Hemings had children together.

Conversations with the elders hold special keys that are available few other places to from whence you come. One person armed with pertinent information that their ancestor did not cook with fire but hot stones identified an African place of origin.

Another person collected information, that grandmother snuck up behind their grandchildren on their birthdays and greased their nose, pointed to origins in Africa. Some others have found that African naming practices, a burial song, and folklore existed. Do not delay taking out time to rap with your elders.

Collecting pieces of the African story, which were held by various branches of his family, has communicated the importance of paying close attention to conversations with our elders for genealogist Karim Aldridge Rand. More than twenty years ago, he had little, if any, experience in the art of interviewing. He managed to gather through cross interviewing that his Great-great Grandfather Alan Williams was a "pure African."

In recent times, the oral tradition in its fullness presented itself when he was surprised to receive a great aunt's obituary that made reference to his forefather as a Yoruba, though he was not fortunate enough to have ever met or spoke with her. Still, this information helped to shed light upon "why after all had he such a strong affinity for Ifa'Orisa (Yoruba Spirituality) for all these years?"

Twelve Tips For Interviewing

Genealogist Robert H. Williams discovered his connection to Benjamin Banneker through oral history. For more than ten years, genealogist Karim Aldridge Rand now has possessed the skills to conduct research into oral traditions. He credits Wendell Wray, former director of the Schomburg Center, who taught a course "Oral History/Tradition" in which he enrolled for his wealth of knowledge. Experienced family history researchers share twelve interviewing tips.

Prepare for your interview

"Now, components of a good oral history are grounded in preparation." Rand emphasizes.

The first step calls for getting a handle on the topic that you are to explore. You might do some background reading on the times that your candidate to interview lived.

Similarly, find out what you can about the elder before you schedule your first interview. You might find out what their likes and dislikes are, what their interests are, and how best to conduct yourself.

"It is very important to secure the signature of the informant in the form of an Oral History Agreement Form." Genealogist Karim Aldridge Rand recommends. "The agreement should outline the specifics, conditions and use of the end product (the physical taped interview and the hardcopy transcript)."

Armed with this information, it will help with the introductions, the conversation flowing, and drafting of questions. Questions should be open-ended that will not produce a simple "yes" or "no" response. You want to get the elder talking.

Your background research should help you to know what types of items someone might have. Ask specific questions about the availability of documents. It is always good to ask, "Do you have any or know the whereabouts of any of the following?"

▼ photos,
▼ family Bibles,
▼ diaries,
▼ letters,
▼ awards,
▼ farm records,
▼ baptismal records,
▼ wedding albums,
▼ funeral home programs,
▼ diplomas,
▼ marriage licenses,
▼ employment records,
▼ yearbooks,
▼ military service records

Select Quality Equipment

"The selection of the media to use—tape recorder or video camera or both—deserves careful consideration." Karim Alridge Rand notes.

(Note: depending on availability, be courteous and ask your informant if she wouldn't mind if you videotaped the sessions.)

And if you plan to conduct a telephone interview, use a mild to high-end telephone recorder (the same would apply for all equipment you use). Whatever you decide, make sure that it is functional as well as operational. Hence test the equipment thoroughly before your interview session.

I have used both micro-cassette recorders and full-size recorders with success. I personally prefer the full-size recorder based solely upon adaptability. Voices on my older full-size tapes have become faded with time, though I have used improved high-end recorders to enhance the clarity.

I finally recommend taking backup notes during the interview and ask permission to take a photograph. Trust me, even quality equipment fails, every now and then. So jot down a few notes.

Get Rid of All Preconceived Notions

I personally have found that a mental adjustment sometimes is necessary for my interview to be a success. Practice active listening. This means listen oh so carefully to what the elders are telling you.

"Try and establish a rapport with your informant before you begin interviewing, especially if your informant is an elderly person or someone you don't know personally," Rand suggested.

Bring a Memory Jogger

An old photo of family gathering or a familiar place out of the past, church souvenir book, and scrapbook are good ways to jog memories and get a conversation going.

"It is important that we interview the senior citizens and help them to label their photographs. If you look around my office, you'll notice I have many photographs of people." Charles L. Blockson, author of *Black Genealogy* noted.

"Sure they are beautiful, but there are no names to attach to the faces. On a rainy day we should take the time to identify photographs, so that ten years hence someone will know who the individuals are."

Relax and Blend In

Family members in the South always told the best stories before or after a meal. So I learned to anticipate taking time out to eat and socialize.

If you are uncomfortable or tense, your subject will surely pick up on it. So limber up! You will be surprised at how well things go simply by being yourself. First and foremost, relax, most people are happy to have someone sit and intently listen to their stories.

Provide Positive Feedback and Take A Nonjudgmental Posture

Try and give positive nonverbal cues, such as a nod or smile that says "I'm with you." I learned this the hard way.

"What was your father's name?" I sat with pen and paper ready to capture my mother's words and asked.

"Nathaniel, Ethaniel, Etania, E.S., Joe." She was rattling off. She then caught my look of puzzlement and didn't like. She threw her hands up in the air.

"Why, I don't know what his name was? And I don't know if this is a good idea!"

It later was that I understood that my mother came of age in a time when children were to be seen and not heard. Remember, there are bound to be things uncovered that were both notable and less than glamorous in your family history.

Don't Challenge Through Verbal or Nonverbal Cues What An Elder Tells You

I recommend interviewing one family member at a time, alone if possible. I made the error of interviewing three siblings one. It was hard to figure out who said and what. What was clear that there were differences of opinion about what happened, when, where, and clearly why.

"Learn as much as you can about your family history from as many relatives and their friends as you can. Some will have different versions of the same thing." Genealogist Robert H. Williams shares pearls of wisdom. "Don't argue with them about their version, or take sides with someone whose version you like. Instead, listen and take down what they tell you."

Don't Interrupt

Some people have rehearsed the way they tell a story. Good storytellers tell their stories in a sequence of events. So anticipate periods of silence, but don't interrupt. It is told in a particular sequence of events and interruption breaks the chain and train of the thought. Wait for a follow-up visit to check out what information you missed.

I was interviewing one elder Silas Askerneese when I asked him a question about what he just had said. He responded "now I lost my place" and got to start over.

Be Considerate

Be considerate of the time. Stick to your initial time allotment, for in the end both parties will be satisfied. Plan for three sessions (sixty to ninety minutes each) to do a thorough job. Other arrangements can be made, if deemed necessary.

"Ask the participant, if need be, could you do any follow up interviews for further clarification." Karim Aldridge Rand says.

Call or write as a simple reminder to confirm the follow-up interview. Come dressed suitable for the occasion.

Bring a small token of your appreciation. It can be a souvenir from the family reunion to some other item they might like to the follow-up interview. I have given copies of family photos to copies of publications about the family. Finally, don't and forget to send a thank you note after the interview.

Don't Procrastinate

"Be prepared to conduct oral interview via telephone, if necessary." Genealogist Karim Aldridge Rand urges.

I personally have invested almost one hundred fifty dollars in a voice-activated telephone cassette recorder after a person I was scheduled to visit in person passed before I was able to make the trip to Georgia. The voice-activated feature allows for discontinuance of taping after a long pause, avoiding long blank spaces on the cassette. The tape recorder has been one of my best research equipment investments, as it doubles as a regular cassette recorder and telephone cassette recorder.

Time is not waiting on anyone. Now is the time to get started, talking to your elders.

Record Your Source

Genealogist Robert H. Williams advises. "Either by using a tape recorder, by mail, or over the telephone, always record the following: How you received the information, from whom, and the date? This is your source."

Transcribe Tapes

Oral history helps in answering answer who, where (town, county, state), when, how and sometimes why. Transcribing is the time consuming process of writing down in hard copy format what was said in the interview sessions. A hard copy will provide an easy point of reference in helping to locate documents that will enhance your family history in the future.

Florence Bridges, hostess of Pittsburgh's Wisdom Years along with the author on televisions show.

Faith Ruffin Davis, National President of the Afro-American Historical and Genealogical Society (center), presents charter to Gladys Nesbit (left) and the author, Western Pennsylvania AAHGS co-founders at Towson Maryland AAHGS Conference.

Mr. Barksdale-Hall presenting "Finding Your Roots" session at the National Council of Negro Women Black Family Reunion, National Mall, Washington, D.C.

The Interview

Schedule your appointments in a comfortable place with little background interference. It typically is a good idea to plan for at least three meetings. Organizing for a successful oral history project calls for preparation.

"Take into account the interview context in framing his questions and appropriately tailored questions based on the subject matter." Rand adds. "As a rule, though, he began with general questions, gradually moving to specific questions."

Now, you are prepared to make the initial contact and discuss the purpose of your planned interview. For help with autobiographical questions, look at Barbara Ann Kipfer's *4,000 Questions for Getting to Know Anyone and Everyone* (Random House Reference 2004). Interviews can be autobiographical, thematic, or a mixture of the two.

The interviewer can provide a brief introduction to the interview session. The lead can include your name, the date, time, location of the interview, and a brief statement of the purpose for the interview. The following is a short list of sample thematic questions for genealogical, family history research of an individual, compiled with the assistance of genealogist Karim Aldridge Rand.

Sample Interview Questions

Full name and place of birth of informant, including parents, brothers, and sisters

1. Would you please state your full name at birth?

2. Would you please spell your name?

3. Did you have a nickname?

4. If so, what was it?

5. How do you spell your nickname?

6. Which name did you or your family use most frequently?

7. How did you acquire this nickname?

8. What did your nickname mean?

**Full names and places of birth
of informant's parents and grandparents, if possible**

1. What are the names of your mother and father?

2. Where was your mother born and raised?

3. Where was your father born and raised?

4. Do you remember any of your grandparents?

Significant childhood-adolescent experiences

1. Where did you attend elementary, junior high and high school?

2. What was your favorite subject in school?

3. Did you participate in any extracurricular activities?

4. Who was your favorite teacher?

Significant historical and/or social events that possibly impacted interviewee's life and others

1. What do you remember about the Montgomery Bus Boycott in Alabama

2. Do you remember when President Kennedy was assassinated?

3. Was your father a World War One veteran

4. When did your parents leave the South?

5. Why did they migrate to Pennsylvania?

The role of social institutions

1. What's the name of the oldest Black Church in your community?

2. Was there a black business association?

3. What Masonic groups or fraternities/sororities were active in the community?

4. Were there any black cemeteries?

When I interviewed my seventy-something uncle, who was an Elk, he shared these comments about his life and times:

> *Most all of the people belonged to the Elks. That was the biggest thing going. After the Elks moved… Well they had quite a few members where they were at, but when they moved from there to where they are now that was the biggest thing around there, the Elks. That was the biggest name you heard around here. You didn't hear anything else… Charles Vactor was a big politician.*

> *When they had Vactor as exalted ruler, they built that building [gymnasium] next to the Elks…From Friday night you caught the devil there because that place was loaded down up there, because I worked on the bar. There were four of us on the bar and a dishwasher and buddy we'd be running…*

> *Oh we had money then. You see J. Finley Wilson was the grand exalted ruler and he'd travel all over the country telling the people if you want to see somebody with money go to Farrell that little town had money. Bought a bus had our own bus… We went to conventions, ball games, and everywhere with the bus. Like I said we were the only lodge around in this country that had things like that.*

I always had pictured my uncle as quiet and staid, watching television or on the porch. Yet you catch an exciting glimpse of his heyday.

I asked around about the Elks and before long had interviewed twenty folks. Organized in 1914, the Twin City Elks Lodge was recognized for almost twenty years as the largest Independent and Benevolent and Protective Order of Elks of the World (IBPOEW) lodge in Pennsylvania.

Reaching a cross section of African-Americans in Farrell, an industrial town, the African-American organization was a powerful unifying force in the community. I just was unprepared for what thrill awaited. In 1993, I received a historical award from The Pennsylvania Historical and Museum Commission for my research on this fraternal group.

Indeed, I was left with a lasting impression of the positive role played by African-Americans, if sometimes overlooked, in community building. The conversation with your elders can be an eye opener.

Life Application

1. Who would be candidates to interview in your family?

2. What African-American organizations are serving the entire community welfare today?

3. What vital role, if any, has African-American social institutions played in community building in your hometown?

4. In recent times what events have significantly impacted your life?

5. How can African-American's institutions better serve the entire community in present times?

Chapter Five
Making a Slave

In recent times, students and teachers in urban school districts have asked about slavery. Making a slave was first and foremost an economic concern. As slave narratives and documents support, the bottom line was turning a profit. Granted it was a messy business for sure.

Challenge the myth that "slavery was not so bad." Believe you me, the myth is out there. In recent times I have heard it stated from educators in some urban communities.

Here are a few tips to challenge the myth.

▼ Show the uninformed a photo of enslaved African Gordon's scarred back found on page 17 of Velma Maia Thomas's *Lest We Forget: The Passage from Africa to Slavery and Emancipation* (Crown Publishers 1997).

▼ Outline how slaves were made.

▼ Share the following reading list on "making a slave." For scholarly readings, see twentieth century historians Ira Berlin's *Many Thousands Gone: The First Two Centuries of Slavery in North America* (1998), Eugene Genovese's *Roll, Jordan, Roll* (1974), and Kenneth M. Stampp's *The Peculiar Institution* (Knopf 1956).

▼ Read and tell the story of Linda Brent or Frederick Douglass.

How were slaves made? The findings are provocative. My people's enslavement developed over a span of several decades. In 1619, twenty Africans from Angola arrived off the coast of Virginia, beginning what has been a great encounter that has spanned three hundred plus years. My people's first Americans were indentured servants. By

1640 my people were being considered permanent servants and the condition inherited by offspring in Virginia.

One of the most concise definitions of a slave can be found in the 1825 *Louisiana Civil Code*:

▼ A slave is one who is in the power of a master to whom he belongs. The master may sell him, dispose of his person, his industry, and his labor: he can do nothing, possess nothing, nor acquire anything but what must belong to the master.

▼ Primary conditions of slavery included permanency and inheritability.

Slave Management

Judge John Ray of Georgia (1793-1868) acquired considerable material gains in the form of real estate and my people. He addressed the role of the white overseer, who was a sort of foreman with the responsibility of overseeing the day-to-day plantation operations, in making a slave. He was the author of following article, which appeared in *The Carrollton Times*.

Rules for the Treatment of My Slaves by the Overseers

The Overseer must keep his temper in check; never whip in a passion; control his passions at all times.

All hands must obey the Overseer in all matters in and about the plantation and work—must not disobey orders given, must do the work as directed, must not be impudent.

Must not quarrel among themselves, must not steal, kill hogs, injure stock, nor leave fences down; must have all the tools forthcoming, let none be lost; when done using a tool, put it in its proper place.

All hands must sweep their houses at night before they lie down, bring in fresh water and throw out the dirty water, must retire to bed at ten o'clock every night unless kept up by the order of the overseer or by special business.

Must not leave the plantation without permission at any time—except on Saturday nights those who have wives will be permitted to visit them, but must return in time to do a full day's work, at least a half-hour after sunrise, the Overseer to be the judge, and if one comes too late, on thee second or third time he must come back on Sunday night.

The married men must feed on Sunday in turn.

The other hands must not leave the plantation until after breakfast on Sunday morning and must return between seven and eight o'clock in the evening. If the weather is bad, must not leave without the permission of the overseer and a pass.

Must wash and patch their clothes once a week and keep them in good order.

The woman at the house must sun all the bedclothes once in two weeks at least, on the fence, and bring them in before sunset or in case of rain. In good weather the doors and windows of their houses must be left open in order to air them.

Must not steal from each other or any other person.

Must feed and curry the mules carefully and must not throw sticks or stones at them when they attempt to catch them.

If any negro should resist the overseer when he goes to whip one, he is call on two or three of the men to tie him and they must obey promptly.

Women and boys are not to get more than fifteen to twenty-five lashes with the strap—or small switches—to whiten the skin, but in no case to cut the skin; never giving more than ten lashes at a time without stopping a minute or two and talking to the negro, then resuming the whipping—if necessary—until humble, and he promises to do right, then take him or her on this promise.

Never scuffle or run after a negro, if possible they must obey and stand and not resist at any time, if they do it shall be worse with them at all times.

All punishment must be increased or diminished as thee circum-stance of the case seem to require in order to maintain good order and government in all matters, and for all persons.

Hands must not be worked in a down-pouring rain that will wet them if possible to prevent—particularly the women.

In the short days give them about three-quarters of an hour to eat, but an hour in the long days from the time they get to the house till they leave, and the same when they eat in the field.

See that their bread is well cooked and do not let them waste it. Make them sift the meal clean.

When the negroes see a rail down, require them in passing to put it up and draw bars, gates and water-gaps kept in good order to keep the stock out of the fields.

Require the sheep feeder, the ox feeder, the cattle feeder, and the mule feeders to do their duty regularly, with economy and care; see to it yourself, and that they report the condition of all the stock. Keep a little corn in the pens for the small pigs through the day; have the sheep seen to every day,—give them sometime a little oats, cotton-s-eed, fodder or salt, of a night to make them come up more readily.

Burn the beds of the hogs, change the plan of feeding if necessary, if mangy or lousy give them brimstone and copperas occasionally.

Whip (the negroes) on the legs and thighs and butt, but never on the back; never be cruel, but be obeyed, and govern firmly and promptly—Make them love and obey you. When they do well, encourage them and show you are pleased; keep them in good heart and spirits and stimulate them, be at their work.

Require all work to be well done, make them lap the furrows, break close and well and break new dirt every time, do not let the plow hands lose time at the end of rows, but lift the plough around. Don't let them be jerking the mules as it will injure them. Make them plough up to the bank of the ditches and the side of them into the corners of the fences.

Be always with the hands when at work and go from hand to hand. Keep the gin and plough and tools in good order and let no one do bad work, keep them working at full speed. Keep your thought ahead of your work, and your work planned out for dry weather, and for wet weather, in order that no time be lost. Wet days let Simon work in the shop, and Wiley and you upon plough stocks, harrows, how handles and other tools.

Burn a large coal kiln; make Simon tend it to have it well done, attended to night and day. Start the fire on a Monday and it will be burned that week.

Farm Journals and the social pages of the day regularly ran features about "making a slave." The society pages published under the listing, management of slaves, provocative articles written by John Ray and other prominent planters.

Making a Slave and Resistance

The first and second generations of my people generally were openly defiant. There were those who fought. Some seized slave vessels. Others committed suicide. Enslaved Africans tended to runaway in small groups in hopes of establishing maroon societies in swamps and secluded reaches.

There is very little praiseworthy to be said on "making a slave." As earlier mentioned, surprisingly, I have heard an erroneous view expressed by some unenlightened educators in recent times. The

73

myth is that "slavery was not so bad." I put together Ten Rules for Making a Slave for the layperson to help you in discussion of the slave making business.

Ten Rules for Making a Slave

▼ **Inflict Deep Psychological Scarring**

Deep psychological scarring was slavery's enduring legacy. Captors desired to generate fear of quick and swift reprisals to discourage rebellion. They struck fear into the heart of my people with the tools of psychological torture, which included murder, rape, maiming, lynching, burning at the stake, and deprivation of food, clothing, and creature comforts.

Once my people were exposed to these atrocities, the news spread like wildfire. Deep psychological scarring was the outcome, which entered into my people's family systems and was passed on. Through the informal grapevine the enslaved communities heard of these atrocities and passed the stories on.

Enslaved ancestor's breaking in process called for beatings into a stupor, again and again. Beatings left physical scars, which were not minimal. We selected as a reminder the enslaved ancestor Gordon's scarred back to grace the cover of Jah Kente International's "Redemption Ritual Inviting the Ancestors to be Present" program held at the Frederick Douglass National Historic Site in Washington, DC on August 31, 2001.

Read Solomon Northup's narrative *Twelve Years a Slave: Narrative of Solomon Northup, a Citizen of New-York, Kidnapped in Washington City in 1841, and Rescued in 1853* for a description of the breaking in process.

▼ **Disrupt Communication Lines**

Slave laws in Barbados prohibited my people's playing of drums. In the American colonies slave laws were passed to restrict the use of talking drums, which provided an effective way to communicate news from one plantation to another. Restrictions upon public gatherings further limited the transmission of knowledge. My people were not permitted to speak their Mother tongue, which was being loss by the third and fourth generation except in secluded regions on the Sea Islands.

▼ Forbid Learning To Read or Write

Our great liberator Frederick Douglass secretly taught slaves at a Sabbath School, though slave codes expressly forbid teaching slaves how to read or write. A few clever mulattoes, life Frederick, were taught by their parents, mistresses, or children. Frederick Douglass gained the basic ABC's from his master's wife, who unwittingly taught him.

She later made aware of the "wrong" of teaching slaves, attempted to frustrate his effort for more education on. There were a few Sabbath schools, though nine out of ten of the African-American masses remained illiterate upon freedom.

Captors expressed an unwillingness to instruct my people in their preferred form of communication, the written word. Read Thomas Webber's *Deep Like the Rivers: Education in the Slave Quarter Community* (W.W. Norton 1978) to learn how enslaved communities passed on knowledge and culture through storytelling, secret church meetings and other means.

▼ Devalue a People's Past

My people had a glorious past. Ethiopians were esteemed in antiquity. Great civilizations included Mali, Ghana, Songhay, and Carthage. Libraries existed in Timbuctoo and Carthage.

Captors devalued Africa's glorious past. They mocked my people for their earth-tone skin, thick lips, wide nostrils, kinky hair, and voluptuous behinds. My people re-identified themselves with their captor when then were stripped of their language, traditions, and culture.

▼ Teach the Myth of the Captor's Superiority

The Chesapeake Region, which included Virginia and Maryland, was a slaving center. In 1676, a show of support from enslaved Africans, who one out of ten participated in Bacon's rebellion, what was said to be an English class, signaled a warning to wealthy whites. The alarm was over the cooperation between mistreated European indentured servants and enslaved Africans in Virginia. European indentured servants were being underfed and overworked.

What was the white aristocracy to do? The planters studied the problem. A concern about European indentured complaints, getting back to their homeland, was real. However, little likelihood of complaints about slavery getting back to Africa existed. Who did enslaved Africans have to appeal for legal redress after all? Planters arrived with an answer. A greater wedge was to be drawn between whites of all classes and my people!

Wealthy planters fired back and began to place greater emphasis upon racial differences rather than class, promoting the myth of white superiority. White indentured servants, poor whites, and white females all were to feel superior to my people. The strategy was tied to a decrease in the reliance of indentured white servants and increase in the importation of Africans. A wedge was driven between poor whites and my people. The strategy effectively worked.

▼ **Foster an Atmosphere of Division**

The Willie Lynch speech, broadcasted at the Million Man March in 1995, probably is best known for how to make a slave. White aristocrats used a method of divide and conquer, again and again. The greatest of all strategies for diffusing unrest was to pit one slave against the other: the slaves vs. overseers; house slave vs. the field slave; dark skinned vs. mulatto; and country vs. urban.

▼ **Afford No Legal Protection To Marriage and The Family**

The separation of families for my people, who were communal and family loving, was one of the greatest fears. Pauli Murray, who authored a family account *Proud Shoes* (Harper and Rowe 1956) tells how captor Sidney Smith had the power to dissolve her enslaved ancestor Harriet and free person of color Reuben

Day's marriage. Lustful Smith then was at liberty to fulfill his sexual desires with her, which he did. Any marriage involving an enslaved partner, if it was between either a free person of color or another enslaved person, was afforded no legal protection. Noticeably absent from the pronouncement at all slave wedding ceremonies was "until death do you part."

▼ Pass Slave Status On Through the Mother

Chattel or moveable property, like livestock, became the accepted slave status of my people. Lustful captors often raped my people's women. To boot the offspring was about two hundred dollars in the captor's pouch. For an enslaved woman's perspective on these sexual advances, read Linda Brent's *Incidents in the Life of a Slave Girl* and Jean Fagan Yellin's *Harriet Jacobs: A Life*.

In *Proud Shoes* planter Mary Ruffin Smith listed her mulatto nieces, who born to both of her brothers and an enslaved woman Harriet, on the 1860 census as chattel, also known as moveable property. The captors came to physical blows over the beautiful Harriet. Mary Smith's nieces, who remained inheritable property, were at risk of sale and the associated risk of sexual exploitation and rape when and if the Smiths died.

The condition of slavery that the enslaved status of a mother was inheritable gave my people's women few avenues out. This represented an exception to British law, which had held that a child followed the status of their father.

▼ Reorient to Captor's World View and Interests

My people boasted in what their captor possessed, though captors held out few carrots. Some gave a dress or hat or an increase in the food allotment for a newborn. Others promised freedom for certain work. As Sojourner Truth found the promises were sometimes empty. She met her end of such a deal for freedom and then her captor reneged. All hope of continued enslaved family and community life as it remained centered upon the economic success of the plantation.

My people lacked few, if any, material possessions and had a total dependence upon their captors. From the early eighteenth century up until the American Revolution, Elias Ball, a large plantation owner in South Carolina, provided token cash incentives to increase slave production. In 1740, a female slave received two pounds and fifteen shillings from tobacco grown on her personal assigned patch, though it was not enough to purchase her freedom.

▼ **Create the Myth of the Happy Slave**

Captors circulated the "Myth of the Happy Slave." My people amazingly withstood such an onslaught and still have laughter. Frederick Douglass tells the story of an enslaved African, who complained about hardship—not being fed enough—and was sold away from the family. Interestingly, through laughter my people coped with the absurdity of the slave world. Laughter was a mask to release pent up emotions, take a jab at unequal status, and to reconstruct my people's fragile existence.

International Sons and Daughters of Slave Ancestry

Where there is no struggle, there is no progress, our liberator Frederick Douglass championed. International Sons and Daughters of Slave Ancestry (ISDSA), a non-profit lineage society, have a stirring philosophy, which promotes "pride in our enslaved ancestors" and sets out to "remember the past, not erase it."

I have exhibited as part of the International Sons and Daughters of Slave Ancestry's "A Tribute to Our Enslaved Ancestors" at the DuSable Museum in Chicago. What a wonderful celebration of my people! Beautiful heirloom quilts of enslaved ancestors graced the great hall, the story of my people's struggle finally being celebrated.

Anybody, who wants to get in on the buzz about reparations, better beware. You first will have to struggle. Documenting your descent from an enslaved ancestor is a must before collecting a dime. How can you trace your slave ancestors and better be prepared to collect?

To have your research certified by a lineage society possibly can put a little jingle in your pocketbook, as I hope to find.

The International Society of Sons and Daughters of Slave Ancestry (ISDSA)
PO Box 436937
Chicago, Illinois 60643-6937
ISDSA@aol.com
www.rootsweb.com/~ilissdsa

Mr. Barksdale-Hall with Robert H. Williams, co-founder of the International Sons and Daughters of Slave Ancestry (ISDSA), view panels for Wilson Steverson at the Tribute to Our Enslave Ancestors exhibit, DuSable Museum, Chicago, Illinios.

ISDSA maintains a slave archival database, publishes a newsletter, and promotes education through a traveling exhibit, "A Tribute to Our Enslaved Ancestors." Certified membership, based upon documented lineage to a slave ancestor, is open to any individuals without regard to sex, race, color, creed, or national origin.

Upon your application for membership you will receive a list of "sources acceptable as proof," including primary, secondary, and other supporting documents. Well, tracing slave ancestors can be done, but it promises to be something else!

Life Applications

1. How might you now challenge the myth that "slavery was not so bad?"

2. What, if any, relevance does the Ten Rules for Making a Slave have to present times?

3. How in light of the readings would you evaluate slavery as an economic concern?

4. How in light of the readings do you view the present-day call for reparations? Would you apply if money became available? Why?

5. Please place in a priority list (from 1 to 10, with 1 being the most important) the Ten Rules for Making a Slave, as to the seriousness of these strategies to the long term effect upon the development of family and community life. Why did you rank in this order?

Chapter Six
Tracing Slave Ancestors

What fury had I unleashed? It started out pleasant enough with an update on our research. The reference to the Confederacy however struck a nerve. Some family bristled at the notion that Great Grandfather Wilson Stevenson, a body servant, served alongside his master George R. G. Fambrough in the Civil War.

"Why didn't he run away?" "Dumb nigger" was overheard. Others held there was no such thing in the world as a good slave owner. Simply put, all masters were vile, lecherous, greedy, and suspicious characters at best. Now, all African-Americans supposedly knew that. So what was up? My mother warned me to let the past be. I now was in the middle of a conflict. I was on the grill and feeling the heat. Folk was looking to me for answers. At that moment I had none beyond hat—give the man a break, he was a slave.

Greater Love Has No One

Greater love has no man than this that he lay down his life for his friend, I recalled. It was through my contact with Ken how I learned that former Marse George R. G. Fambrough was shot through a window and killed as he defended a former slave's life. Information on this event came through an unexpected source. I received a blind mailing from a descendant of Moore Stephenson, who owned my Stevenson ancestors.

Oral history said ancestors Archie and Harriet chose the surname Stevenson after their "kind masters," though to our generation the word "kind master" smarted of step and fetch it, paternalism, and Uncle Tom. Written records provide background on the origins of the name Steverson. The issue was addressed by the Youngstown

[Ohio] Vindicator, in commemorating the birthday of my great grandfather Wilson Steverson.

Mr. Wilson Stevenson is the only one of Pennsylvania's residents to be born in slavery. He is one of a family of 14 children born of Archie and Harriet who were slaves on a Stevenson plantation in Newman, Ga. He says his parents, being without a family name, adopted the name of their kind master after they were made free.[1]

Now, the new findings tested what ideas I held about slavery. And maybe the Stevenson family was of some note after all.

I reflected all the more upon Great Grandpa Wilson's willingness to accompany his master to war and how he always said that he "done the right thing." He bragged about his service. "I could piss and run under it before it hit the ground." He was the most capable slave, who was chosen as a trusted bodyservant.

Another Take on Slavery

The slave business deserved another take. Expanded dialogue about the role of slavery in America has potential to hold the key to bridging the racial divide. Perhaps, some reciprocity, which means give and take, existed in the relationships between Wilson and Marse George, which carried over to freedom. There can be no true relationship without give and take in life. For some time I had been cynical about "kind" being associated with master, though I was aware that Wilson maintained friendly ties with the slave-owning Stevensons into freedom.

Now I reflected all the more upon the relationship between Wilson and George during slavery and freedom. Why was Wilson willing to encounter criticism for his devotion to the white Stevensons? Why did Marse George lay down his life for a former slave? Who was the former slave being defended? Could it just possibly have been Great Grandpa Wilson or a family member? I wondered.

I had a thousand and one questions racing through my head. What was the exact connection, if any, between George R. G. Fambrough and the Stevensons? Why was the bond between master and body-servant celebrated throughout southern history? How was the bond developed? Did the bond last beyond slavery?

My research into slave records has increased my cultural awareness. I have spoken across the country about the story of my fascinating slave ancestors. There have been numerous letters of appreciation for but none so heartfelt as the sentiment expressed by Harry E. Whipkey, former State Archivist of Pennsylvania:

This is to express my deep admiration for the excellent presentation, "Tracing Slave Ancestors," provided by you at the 11th Annual Conference on Black History in Pennsylvania... Your talk, applauded for the force and clarity of the delivery and for the humor so expertly interjected, gave firm evidence of your "nuts and bolts" understanding of genealogical research and your ability to interpret such research for academic purposes.

Your session, and this view was shared by many, was one of the major highlights of the Wilkes-Barre meeting. It was delightful. It was interesting. It was educational.

I have counted it all a rewarding experience to research and tell the story. There have been numerous benefits from researching my slave ancestry.

Slave Family Research

I highly recommend that folks read John Hope Franklin's *From Slavery to Freedom* (Knopf 2000) for a good introduction to slavery. David H. Streets' classic *Slave Genealogy: A Research Guide with Case Studies* (Heritage 1986) has offered a smart approach for anyone interested in researching their slave roots. He has directed with court records and federal population schedules to identify slave families living in non-plantation settings. His evaluation of vital records, probates, deeds, court records, and tax lists has simulated a genealogical trek. He has used records from Wayne County, Kentucky as an example of how to bridge the period between freedom and slavery. He has provided three case studies. A simple design, easy-to-use tables, and well-placed understandable charts have contributed to this guide's usefulness.

Check under the state-by-state resources for research guides in your areas. Mary L. Jackson Fears has examined the complexity of slave research in *Slave Ancestral Research: It's Something Else* (Heritage 1995). If our ancestors were engaged in the Underground Railroad, read Wilbur H. Siebert's *The Underground Railroad from Slavery to Freedom* (Ayer 2000), which contained a valuable list of operators, African-American operators being indicated. William Still included valuable biographical sketches of fugitive slaves in *The Underground Railroad* (Johnson Publishing 1970). To look back into slavery has called upon preparation.

Researching Two Families

To research slave ancestry has involved researching two families. I have researched the kinships of my ancestors' slaveowning families. George R. G. Fambrough married Emily Allen. To discover that Emily Stephenson, Emily Allen, and Emily Fambrough were one in the same represented a major research breakthrough. With this knowledge in hand I concluded that Wilson was held solely by members of the slaveowning Stephenson family during slavery.

I solved a major genealogical puzzle using court records. From an article in the Sharon [Pennsylvania] Herald I knew Great Grandpa Wilson fought in the Civil War alongside his master George Fambrough.[2] Up until the time I searched the annual returns of the guardian for Emily Stephenson, I had been unable to establish an exact relationship between the Stephensons and Fambroughs. It was in using court records, which included annual returns for the guardian of Emily Stephenson, that I found answers.

Richard C. Wade Guardian Return 1854

Received of Rick C. Wade Guardian for Emily Allen formerly Emily Stephenson two hundred and fifty dollars for our professional services in filing and prosecuting a bill in equity in Coweta in Superior Court to a successful fine against Newton Allen for a settlement of the property of the said Emily upon her to her sole separate use this

December 30, 1854   Buchanon McKinley Atty at Law[3]

Coweta Co Georgia Court of Ordinary May Four 1860. It appearing to the court that R.C. Wade guardian of Joseph W. Stephenson and Emily Fambro, formerly Emily Stephenson, has fully paid over to and settled... with George Fambro the husband of said Emily for all the property and money held by the said R.C. Wade as guardian of the said Emily and that and that said R.C. Wade has through the ordinary of said County _____ his application for dimission from said Guardianship to be advertised in terms of the law...

W.B. Wilkinson Ordinary[4]

I have juggled slave names and relationships. As earlier mentioned in Chapter One, my slave research had a simple beginning when my mother gave me a gift from the heart. The clipping was titled "Dad Stevenson Celebrates His 109th Birthday Today." It was later when I was further inspired by Dr. Laurence A. Glasco, professor of history at the University of Pittsburgh, that my mother's seed took root. I then began researching my slave ancestry.

The historical record was unclear, though the birthplace of my Great-great Grandmother Harriet likely was Virginia. During the rise of the Cotton Kingdom she was sold from Virginia to Georgia in

the 1820s. Virginia alone exported almost 300,000 slaves beginning in 1830. The trend of mass movement of slaves from the Carolinas and Virginia to Georgia and Alabama was associated with the separation of enslaved black families coupled with the rise of cotton production in the Deep South. Maryland, North Carolina and Virginia where the soil was depleted sent slaves to the cotton district. Virginia alone exported almost 300,000 slaves beginning in 1830.

Between 1810 and 1820 the black population in Georgia increased from eighty thousand to one hundred thousand; followed by five hundred thousand in the 1860. For example, some slaves from the estate of Moor Stephenson plantation in Georgia remained in Georgia. Others were carried as far west as Texas. Maryland, North Carolina and Virginia where the soil was depleted sent slaves to the cotton district.

Slavery appeared on the decline by the time of the American Revolution, which democratic values led to discussion about slavery. Military service in the Revolutionary War opened the door to a steady flow of manumissions for a season. Pennsylvania led the way of northeastern states with passage of laws for gradual emancipation in 1780.

Freeing of slaves occurred at twenty-eight years-old, when the normal lifetime lasted about forty years. The free African-Americans in Pennsylvania increased from almost 6,500 in 1790 to 38,000 in 1830. Economic issues, invention of the cotton gin, and demand for cotton unfortunately spread slavery through the deep southern states. The result led to separation of families.

Slaves were considered like property, much like livestock, and listed in estate records. Since slaves were valuable property, detailed records were kept in farm journals. Some of these records are in private hands, historical societies, special collections, archives, and libraries.

A Place Called Home

Research of slave family records in Georgia put me on footing with celebrities. Another more notable black family has also uncovered roots in Coweta. Celebrity Lena Horne has roots in Georgia. In *The Hornes: An American Family* Gail Lumet Buckley, daughter of Lena Horne, traces the black Calhouns to Sinai Reynolds, the author's great-great-great-great grandmother. Buckley writes, "Clearly, [the slaveowner] Silas Reynolds had permitted Sinai ("Sinai" or "Siny") and Henry to live alone and earn their own living, which they were probably doing through Sinai's talents as a cook (she was famous for her pies and cakes)."[5] Aunt Synie," as Robert H. Harris of Newnan recalls, "sold [us] gingercakes and persimmon beer."[6]

Realizing that each genealogical experience has its uniqueness, this case study has offered to shed light on understanding the changes that occurred in one particular family do to slavery. Unlike other counties where the ravages of war and /or courthouse fires have destroyed records, severing precious links to the past, in Coweta County slave family records do exist.

Records pertaining to the black Calhouns, Reynolds, Steversons, and Berrys are readily available for research. Bridging the gap between slave and free, the slave family records of Coweta County are a valuable genealogical/historical resource. This case study has showed examples of the available records and provided suggestions for their use.

I traced my slave ancestors to a place called home. It was the hot, sometimes cold, trail of a combination of record sources that I followed to Coweta County Georgia.

Information was pieced together from federal censuses, oral history, newspaper clippings, and vital records. Federal censuses were taken every ten years, beginning in 1790. The 1870 federal population schedule was the first to list the families of those who were former slaves. Beware in that information collected from newspapers and death records was sometimes incorrect. The information was just as good as the informant. Vital records included birth, marriage, and death records.

Home of Record

I had done my homework. I had prepared blind mailings from national telephone directories. Searching the directories, I found the listings for Steversons and Stephensons in Michigan, Georgia, and Alabama. I specifically targeted the metropolitan areas of Detroit, Atlanta, and Birmingham. I contacted the public library and asked about the extent of their local history and genealogy collections.

County histories were where I first read that Moor Stephenson, an early settler, arrived during the 1820's. Helpful materials available at the public library included family histories, city directories, maps, and clipping files.

In response to my query, the Coweta County Genealogical Society offered valuable assistance. A request for information about my family, known as a query, appeared in a genealogical column "Treetops to Roots."

****

Sample Query - I am a senior at the University of Pittsburgh — I am doing a research project on my family tree — I have traced one line of my family tree back to Newnan, GA in the 1830's.

I am searching for any information available on a George Fambrow. He fought for the Confederate side in Georgia during the Civil War. My maternal great-grandfather, Wilson Steverson, was a slave of George Fambrow. I often found the Steverson name misspelled Stevenson.

Wilson was born in Newnan November 3, 1838 to slaves Archie and Harriet. He was one of 14 children. Wilson fought alongside his master during the Civil War. After being freed he emigrated from Coweta County.

In 1938, Wilson's brother, Dennis Steverson was still living in Newnan at the age of 98.

****

Through this query I established contact with distant relatives and former neighbors of my slave ancestors. The editor of Treetop to Roots had gotten in touch with Dennis' (my Great Grandfather Wilson's brother) great-grandchild and Aaron's (my Great Grandfather Wilson's brother) grandchild and we established contact. James Doster of Claxton, Georgia, who was Great-great Uncle Dennis' white neighbor, provided a surprising account:

> *I read with great interest in the Newnan Times-Herald about your research for some of Dennis Steverson's family.*
>
> *As a boy I knew Dennis Steverson very well.... I have sat by him in his swing on his porch and listened to him talk about his boyhood, about the war between the states. He, too, was a slave and served alongside of his master, a Major Jones... Uncle Dennis as I fondly recall him drove a one horse wagon pulled by an oxen.*
>
> *Dennis told me that his family was separated during slavery. I remember talking to him about when I was a small boy perhaps in 1927 or 1928.*
>
> *He told me he was over a hundred years old in 1929 or 1930. We need to contact the Newnan Times-Herald. They carried pictures and a story of him on what they thought was his 100th birthday. This was in the thirties while I was in school at the GA Tech.[7]*

It had been my understanding that African-Americans and whites were not neighbors in the 1920s, thought the myth stood corrected.

This information, when combined with data, which was gathered from local newspapers in Pennsylvania and Georgia, directed me to specific plantations in Coweta County, Georgia. Some information was not so easy to trace. It took almost fifteen years to locate the article about Great-great Uncle Dennis.

I unsuccessfully scoured *The Newnan Times Herald*. My eyes went buggy looking at reel after reel of microfilm. One day an article, "Newnan Has Slave Time Negro Claiming To Be 115 Years of Age: Dennis Stevenson, Interviewed By *Herald Reporter*, Tells of Old Civil War Days As the Slave of Jim Stevenson," arrived in the mail with a note that "thought you would like this" from a great-granddaughter of Dennis Stevenson. Great-great Uncle Dennis stood six feet tall and had a grey beard. What a wonderful gift from the heart!

From Two We Are Many

Archie and Harriet, had 14 children together during slavery, experienced separation. They were separated from their older children upon their master's death in 1849. Their children were hired out or rented. In 1858, Wilson was hired to L. Leply for $80.00. In 1849, twenty nine slaves from the estate of Moor Stephenson, Coweta County, Georgia, were divided into lots of three or less.

Each lot then assigned a number, which was placed in a hat and distributed by lottery, which led to the separation of Archie and Harriet, and their children. Enslaved families suffered great hardship as no legal protection was afforded slave marriage or families. The couple was separated in later years. Some family members were sold, mortgaged, attached to satisfy debts, and transferred to Texas with the expansion of the Cotton Kingdom. Other family members likely were never seen again, as was common.

Upon the death of Moor Stephenson in 1849, an inventory and appraisal of his estate was made. On page 21 of the General Index to Estates the complete listing of the records pertaining to the estate of Moor Stephenson was found. This record lists twenty-nine slaves, including Archie, Harriet, and family:

Arch, a negro man valued at............. $	650.00
Washington, a negro boy valued at.....	650.00
Nathan, a negro boy valued at...........	500.00[8]
Wilson, a negro boy valued at...........	300.00
Dennis, a negro boy valued at...........	200.00
Harriet, a negro woman & child [Cass]	625.00
Charity, a negro boy.....................	400.00
Susan, a negro girl.......................	125.00[9]

The estate records further explained the circumstances which led up to their separation. I read as Archie and family were placed in lots, numbered, then separated by the cast of lots:

> [T]he names of the distributies…were written on a piece of paper and placed in a hat, the numbers [1 through 9, which represented the groupings of slaves] were written on another piece of paper and put in another hat, the hats were both well shaken, a name was then drawn from the hat containing the numbers – and in that manner continued till all were drawn. The following is the result:

No 2 Lenna Stephenson

No 3 Benjamin Stephenson

No 4 Edward M. Storey guardian for Joseph W. Stephenson

No 5 Edward M. Storey guardian for Emily A. Stephenson

No 2 consists of negroes man Arch and woman Harriet and her child Cass

No 3 consists of negroes man Daniel, boy Dallas, and girl Charity

No 4 consists of negroes man Jacob, boy Andy, and girl Susan

No 5 consists of negro boys Washington, Wilson, and Wiley

No 9 consists of negro man Henry heretofore rec. by Thos. J. Stephenson – and negro boys Mack and Dennis[10]

Probate records told the story of Moor's death and tragic separation of my ancestors.

Approaching the Slave Schedules

I approached the 1850 and 1860 slave schedules with this information in hand. I hoped to combine the names of my slave ancestors with basic physical descriptions (e.g. age and color).

Returning to the inventory and appraisal of Moor's estate in 1849, I established the ages of some slaves based upon comparisons between appraised values and known ages of several slaves, who had already been identified 21 years later in the 1870 federal population schedule. Thus, I was able to establish at minimum an age range for most of the slaves.

Beginning with the 1850 slave schedule, I located the heirs of Moor Stephenson. The 1850 slave schedule listed the household of Linnah Stephenson, widow of the deceased (who in 1840 inherited Archie, Harriet, and Cash):

1850 slave schedule of Coweta County Georgia

Linnah Stephenson

age sex color	age sex color
40 M Mu	6 M Bl
37 F Bl	4 F Bl
33 F Bl	2 F Bl
7 M Bl	2 M Bl

As I identified slave ancestors, these statistics came alive. "Color keys" played a significant role in my research. Using such keys I identified Archie and several of his children. The 40 year old male mulatto on this slave schedule was clearly identified as the slave Archie [the great-great grandfather of the author].

"How was this deduced?" you ask. By simply subtracting 20 years from his age of 63, as recorded in the 1870 federal population schedule, I approximated that Archie would have been about 43 years of age in 1850. Since many slaves did not know their birthdates, variations of 1 to 7 years in recorded age as slaves became adults, were common and were to be expected.

The closer the genealogist with slave ancestry gets to the age of their ancestor during their early years (which covers newborn up to and including 15 years of age), the smaller the range of error becomes for the age of slave ancestors. After comparing various listings and arriving at a rough age for Archie, I uncovered another clue by which to identify Archie and children. In the 1860 and 1870 federal population schedules Archie was listed as mulatto.

My "color key" as was known helped in identifying several of Archie's children. When we consider that most slaveowners in Coweta County and throughout other areas of the South owned 10 slaves or less, then we can realize the possibilities of identifying ancestors on slave schedules with only knowing their color and rough age range. [11]The slave schedules were the earliest available federal records I used. The slave schedules provide masters' manes and physical descriptions (age, color, and sex) of their slaves during the census years of 1850 and 1860.

With the aid of the slave schedule I narrowed down the plantations on which my ancestors were slaves. By now I knew the master's surname. Using that information along with my ancestors physical description from the 1870 population census I skimmed the schedule for slaves fitting my ancestors' descriptions on a plantation owned by a master with that given surname. Eliminating many plantations this method was effective.

Slaves in the Family

More detailed descriptions of ancestors' lives unfolded when information from court records was combined with data from slave schedules. Most of her life Great-great Aunt Charity was held by members of the slaveowning Stephenson family. Several of my slave ancestors were inherited by minor children of the deceased Moor Stephenson. Court appointed guardians oversaw the affairs of these children. In the annual reports of these guardians a wealth of genealogical/historical information was buried.

> Physical descriptions of slaves were found recorded in annual returns:

> Richard C. Wade Guardian for J. W. Stevenson
> No 18

> Recd of RC Wade my guardian three negroes Jake about twenty three years old Andy about eighteen years of age both of dark complexion and Susan about twelve years of age light-complexion being all the negroes the said guardian had of mine in his possession Sept – 18th 1856

> J. W. Steverson[12]

> Property transferals (of which slaves were included) were recorded in annual returns:

Richard C. Wade Guardian Return 1854
Voucher No 1

Received of RC Wade Guardian of Emily Stephenson
the sum of one thousand and sixty one dollars and
twenty five cents including interest in full consideration
for a certain negro girl of yellow complexion called
Charity about fourteen years old when sold and for
which I made and delivered a bill of sale for said negro
to the said Wade as Guardian for the said Emily
Stephenson as aforesaid, February 25, 1855

$1061.25Cts   D.L. Thomas[13]

In 1849 Charity was inherited by Emily Stephenson's brother
Benjamin F. Stephenson. She appears to have been sold or lost during
the intervening years between 1849 and 1855. However, the above
document reveals that Charity was purchased by Emily Stephenson
in 1855, thereby returning Charity to the hands of the slaveowning
Stephenson family.

Some slaves stayed in the family, though it did not negate the risk of
rape and mistreatment associated with renting slaves, commonly
referred to "hiring out." The annual returns provided a record of
"hiring out" for the Stephenson slaves. Charity like the other slaves
(including my great grandfather Wilson) who were owned by Emily
Stephenson were "hired out." "[T]he hiring out of slaves, with its
attendant uncertainties" was one such risk taken by the new owner.[14]

By 1858, everyone had been "hired out." For $80.00 Wilson was
hired to L. Leply; for $130.00 Washington was hired to W. Carmical;
and for $50.00 Charity was hired to Thomas Covington.[15] The
income generated, was used to pay for Miss Emily' tuition to the
Newnan Academy, a private school, clothing, and other expenses.

Washington (ca. 1832-1921) and Sidney Kellogg were founders of Newnan Chapel Methodist Episcopal Church, Newnan, Georgia; in a photo taken in the early 1900s. Washington Kellogg, artisan and former slave, was great-grandfatheer Wilson Stevenson's eldest brother.

Heir Property

From a published history of the Stephenson family I learned that the grandfather of Moor Stephenson died in Greene County Georgia.[16] At the Georgia Department of Archives and History I scoured indexes of estate records for Greene and other neighboring counties.

In the Franklin County index, I found an entry for the estate of William Stephenson. In his will Moor Stephenson, who was the sole son of the deceased, was listed as receiving one negro slave Jack, a colt, land, plus the majority of his father's remaining assets.[17]

Exploring the possibility that earlier generations of the slaveowning Stephenson family held my ancestors, I traced their roots to see if my ancestors might have been received as wedding gifts or heir property.

Between guardianship and tax records I established that at an early age Moor was already financially secure. In 1802 the Negro boy Jack was "hired out" for 46 dollars.[18] By 1818 Moor Stephenson owned 486 acres in Franklin County.[19] I also researched the Hardin ancestry of Linnah Stephenson. Using the records of the Georgia Department of Archives and History facilitated my research of new communities.

Taking the Challenge On

In *Black Genealogy* Charles L. Blockson recounted tracing his family back into slavery. So on a visit to the Charles L. Blockson Collection at Temple University I caught up with him and asked, "What is the likelihood of others achieving similar success?"

"I've met people, some from the Afro-American Historical and Genealogical Society, including yourself, who have had some luck in doing that, but it is a difficult task." While Charles L. Blockson offers a word of caution. "Alex Haley did it. It is possible, but I wouldn't depend too much upon that, because it is very difficult to go back. Nevertheless, you should go back as far as you can."

Tracing slave ancestors remains a challenge worth taking on. All my questions have not been answered, though I feel a sense of creative contentment. As researchers undertake research from both sides of the vast Atlantic Ocean, more sources for slave research continue are anticipated to become available in the future. To follow the winding tracks of our slave ancestors transports us from freedom through slavery to Africa's door.

Life Applications

1. Reflecting upon the reading, what was the legacy of slavery?

2. Reflecting upon the readings, "No Greater Have No One" and "Another Take on Slavery" what applications for the concept of reciprocity, which means some give and take, exist in today's society?

Endnotes

1   "109-Year-Old-Sharonite Born as Slave in Georgia." *Youngstown (Ohio) Vindicator*. 8 February 1948, A-18.

2   *Sharon [PA] Herald*, op. cit.

3   Annual Returns. Book G, p. 289.

4   Minute Book D, p. 238. Ordinary Court, Coweta County, Georgia.

5   Gail Lumet Buckley, *The Hornes: An American Family* (New York: Plume Book, 1986), pp. 14-17.

6   Mary G. Jones and Lily Reynolds, *Coweta County Chronicles* (Easley, S.C.: Southern Historical Press, 1928), 117.

7   Letters from James Doster, 7 Feb. 1982 and 2 March 1982.

8   The evidence supporting the relationship of Nathan, Charity, and Susan to Archie and family is inconclusive.

9   Estate records of Moor Stephenson. Inventory and Appraisement, 2 July 1849. Probabte Court, Coweta County, Georgia.

10   Ibidem.

11   For a discussion of how to trace slave ancestors using primarily the federal population schedules and slave schedules see: Slave Genealogy: A Research Guide with Case Studies by David H. Streets.

12   Annual Returns. Book H, p. 262. Probate Court, Coweta County, Georgia.

13   Annual Returns. Book G, p. 289. Probate Court, Coweta County, Georgia.

14   Genovese, *Roll, Jordan, Roll*, 9.

15   Annual Returns. Book I, Probate Court, Coweta County, Georgia.

16   Jessie McDaniel Hamrick, "The Stephensons of Carroll County, A History of a Family," *The Carroll County (GA) Genealogical Quarterly*, 1:2, August 1980.

17   Minutes, Wills Inventories & C., 15 May 1786 – 6 Sept. 1813, pp. 35-36. Ordinary Court, Franklin County, Georgia.

18   Annual Return, Franklin County, Georgia.

19   Tax digest, Franklin County, Georgia.

Chapter Seven

Looking For Freed Persons

If there is no struggle, there is no progress.
Frederick Douglass, 1857

Well, that old Lincoln was a great, big man. He freed the colored, some folks say.

But heaps of damage already had been done. No stroke of the pen would ever remove. Slavery went on in the minds of the people, leaving a lasting stain on the nation's soul. Reckon, why heaps leftin' to do.

The African-American encounter, which spans 300+ years, can be interpreted through progressing, sometimes declining, degrees of freedom. Prior to 1865 my people, who were not enslaved, lived "quasi-free," an appropriate term coined by the well known historian John Hope Franklin author of *From Slavery to Freedom.* Following the Emancipation Proclamation race relations were slow to change, as hungry colored workers and strapped planter soon realized. One thing at least for sure, the appetite for colored was not soon to subside, if the record of southern dailies were any indicator.

The Dawson Weekly Journal wrote the following.

Custom in civilized countries has rendered it necessary to have a class to take the place of 'hewers of wood and drawers of water'—or servants. African slavery—or the basis of natural inferiority—is the only system that ever worked harmoniously, and the only one that ever will. While the social status of the Negro has been altered... his relationship to the white race, remains virtually the same... our people will embrace and act upon the idea that the Negro is still to raise cotton, corn, etc. though under a different system of labor.

Beyond adversity my people framed a belief and value system. The 1890s of Jim Crow, disfranchisement through poll taxes and grandfather clauses, lynching, and the rise of the KKK ushered in what historians termed a low point in African-American history. DuBois' classic *The Souls of Black Folk* (1903) finally forecasted the problem of the twentieth century to be the "color-line."

"5" Core Values Of Freed People[1]

▼ An Education takes folks somewhere,

"The earnest and touching anxiety of the Freed people to learn, cannot but make a profound impression upon anyone who has the opportunity to observe it. The social and political results of such a change cannot fail to be important." Commanding Major General Pope, highest ranking officer in charge of Florida, Georgia, and Alabama noted in 1867.

Historical Black Colleges and Universities will respond favorably to requests for information about your ancestors' enrollment. Send a self-addressed stamp envelope for reply. Contact the Office of Alumnae Affairs or university archives.

▼ Stewardship of the land,

"Perhaps there could be found no other single index of the results of the struggle of freedmen upward so significant as the ownership of land." The scholar W.E.B. DuBois wrote in 1901.

▼ Sharing, as expressed through a devotion to family and neighbors,

My people did not slaughter a hog without their neighbor's skillet getting a taste. In 1889 Charity Long had fixed on her deed in consideration of the love and affection showed to her together with one dollar was passing on the family homestead.

▼ Commitment to the development of a viable Black Church; sacred and secular institutions,

"I found answers to puzzling questions in church records. Whenever I give lectures at churches, I encourage the membership to preserve their minutes." Charles L. Blockson, author of *Black Genealogy*, says.

▼ Hallmark of industry, as shown through a willingness to work hard and save, realizing every vision of God is a fresh, new opportunity.

The Freedman's Savings and Trust Company had opened ten branches within a year of its inception in 1865; followed with ten additional branches by 1867. The embezzlement of funds, coupled with southern white hostility, was too great of obstacle to overcome. In 1874, the Freedman's Savings and Trust Company closed.

Checklist of Public Records To Look For

▼ Census
▼ Vital Records
▼ Obituaries
▼ Directories
▼ Newspapers
▼ Biographies
▼ Web Sites
▼ Libraries and Archives
▼ County Historical Societies

Census

The 1870 census is the first census that lists my people who had been enslaved, though census takers began with decennial reports in 1790. Debra L. Newman's *List of Free Black Heads of Families in the First U.S. Census of the United States* is a good source for those with free family members in colonial America. Census records, covering from 1790 to 1930, provide a wealth of information. You can find the names of your ancestor, race, occupation, number of children, and more. It is best to start your search with the most current census and work your way back in time.

You can use a helpful index, known as the Soundex System, in locating your ancestors. By all means try and use the Soundex. Using the Soundex I readily located several families that were previously overlooked. Beware, the reporting of information varied over the years. For more detailed information about the census, see Kathleen W. Hinckley's *Your Guide to the Federal Census* (Betterway Books 2002).

My Great-Great Grandparents Archie and Harriet held dual surnames. In the 1870 census we find the following.

Brewster, Archie	[head]	farm laborer	age	63
_____ Harriet	[wife]	keeping house		40
_____ Cass	[son]	farm laborer		21
_____ Laura	[daughter]	at home		14

103

_____ Aaron	[son]	at home		12
_____ Nancy	[daughter]	at home		10
Allen, Noah	[relative of Harriet]	farm laborer		21

Meanwhile the inscription on Harriet's white granite pinnacle-shaped tombstone in Eastview Cemetery reads: Harriet Steveson died Dec. 12 1894, age 75 Our Mother. In his study of the surname selection by freedmen working on the Martin L. Bivins plantation, Kenneth H. Thomas Jr., a historical researcher for the Georgia Department of Natural Resources, concluded, "One family may have multiple surnames rather than a consistent one."[2] My people recognized kinship ties, despite the variations in names.

A well researched study of freedmen's kin-relationships provides a backdrop for exploration of slavery. Carole Merritt, founder of the African-American Family History Association writes,

The most obvious record for reconstruction of the Black family is the federal manuscript census… The 1870 census provides perhaps the most direct access to the slave family just before the Civil War ended…. [For example,] a family of ex-slaves arranged in a single household in 1870 may have five years earlier been a family of slaves divided among two or more plantations due to multiple ownership. The census, then, provides more than individual names. It organizes names into households whose kinship and marriage ties were for he most part established during slavery.[3]

Vital Records

You can obtain the booklet titled *Where to Write for Vital Records: Births, Deaths, Marriages, and Divorces,* from the U.S. Government Printing Office, in Washington, D.C. The state department of health frequently is the custodian of vital records, which include birth, marriage, and death. Check the website of the state department of health.

Obituaries

According to Charles L. Blockson, "Obituaries are very important. Some people save them. Whenever I read in the obituaries of people that I know or who have entered my life, I cut them out. Sometimes these obituaries are of distinguished people, oftentimes they're not. I put them on acid free paper and preserve them here in what is called a vertical file. Obituaries give good vital information."

Directories

Directories will help in pinpointing arrivals and departures from locations. Many events I was told of occurred while family was living at a particular place. I knew where an event occurred, but the directory assisted in identifying when. Business districts and neighborhoods are listed sequentially block-by-block. Older directories' listings included race, names of husband and wife and sometimes older children, employers, occupations, and status of property, if owned or rented. Using older directories, you can begin to reconstruct your ancestor's lives.

Newspapers

My hometown had news items in *The Pittsburgh Courier* and *The New York Age* during the early twentieth century. National editions of African-American newspapers like those along with *The Chicago Defender* had regional correspondents that provided coverage throughout the country. "Colored News" sections with highlights about travel, church and society were carried in majority presses. James M. Rose's *Black Genesis: A Resource Book for African-American Genealogy* (Genealogical Publishing Company 2003) provides state-by-state listing of African-American newspapers, as many smaller African-American newspapers were discontinued.

Putting the Research Together: Case Study

Robert H Williams used various document sources in tracing his Banneker ancestry, much of which having already been cited in 1931 by George Simpson of Wilberforce University. Williams combined information gathered from Bible Records, Census, Vital Records, Cemetery Records along with courthouse records in Ohio, Virginia, and Maryland. An Ohio cousin assisted in sharing research, which he verified. As earlier mentioned, it was through the LETT branch (his maternal line) that he found a connection to Banneker.

The missing documents if they ever existed are:

A. (My sixth great grandparents)—Molly Welsh and Bannka's marriage license. Our oral history says that Molly and Bannka were married. No dates were mentioned. Since miscegenation was unlawful in early Maryland, they may never have gotten a License. At least it has not been found.

B. (My fifth great grandparents)—Mary Banneky and Robert Banneky's marriage license, also not found. Likewise, our oral history says they were married. Being free people of color, they should have been in the records. It is believed that Mary and Robert got married in 1730 since their first child Benjamin Banneker was born on 9 November 1731.

C. (My forth great grandparents)—Jemima Banneker and Samuel Dulaney Lett's marriage document not found either. Again, our oral history said that Samuel Dulaney looked like a white man, and had Indian blood as well. His mother was a white woman. It may be because of his appearance that they were unable to get a license. Again, our oral history stated they were married. Thus far, I have been unable to verify this one way or the other.

The documents Robert H. Williams have are:

A. (My third great grandparents)—Aquilla Lett married Charity Cobbalor on 25 September 1787 in the Evangelical Lutheran Church in Frederick, Maryland. Charity was later known as Christina Cobbler.

B. (My second great grandparents)—John Cummins married Susanna Lett on 25 November 1818 in Harrison County, Ohio.

C. (My first great grandparents)—Joseph Cummins married Esther Lett on 20 September 1860 in Berrien County, Michigan. A notation on the marriage record said: "NIGGERS.

D. (My grandparents)—William J. Hill married Almedia Cummings on 7 November 1887 in Mecosta County, Michigan. Her name was actually Merinda Ann Cummins. She changed her name, and was listed as White. William J. Hill was of Pennsylvania Dutch ancestry, German and French. Merinda Ann Cummins was mixed with Black, White and Red.

Biographies

Robert H. Williams made a point to read as much as he could about his Banneker connection. The Dictionary of American Negro Biography, edited by Rayford W. Logan and Michael R. Winston, published by W. W. Norton & Company, New York – London, copyright 1982, provided an excellent article on Banneker, the information being supplied by Mr. Silvio A. Bedini, a professor emeritus of the Smithsonian Institution in Washington, DC, who also wrote a more definitive biography The Life and Times of Benjamin Banneker.

Popular Sites

▼ **African American Cemeteries Online**

Database of African-American cemeteries with state-by-state listings along with numerous transcriptions. Provides a forum for discussion and queries.
URL: www.prairiebluff.com/aacemetery/

▼ **African-American Genealogy Ring**

A network of approximately 100 sites dedicated to tracing African-American roots
URL: www.afamgenealogy.ourfamily.com

▼ **African American Mosaic**

Selections from the publication, *The African-American Mosaic*. Highlights WPA slave narrative along with images. I found photos of slave narratives and images of quarters from ancestor's home in Eufala, Alabama. The book is available in print.
URL: www.lcweb.loc.gov/exhibits/african/intro.html

▼ **African Ancestry**

Details about DNA testing
URL: www.africanancestry.com

▼ **African American Genealogical Society of Northern California (AAGSNC)**

Library contains almost 1000 links to genealogical sites. Publishes the quarterly newsletter, *From the Boab Tree*.
URL: www.aagsnc.org/

▼ **Afrigeneas**

Discussion, support, and resources are invaluable in helping to get beyond the brick wall of 1870. This is one of the best sites available for tracing African-American roots.
URL: www.afrigeneas.com

▼ **Afro-American Historical and Genealogical Society (AAHGS)**

See for listing of AAHGS affiliates and chapters throughout the country.
URL: www.aahgs.org

▼ **Bibliography of African American Family History at the Newberry Library**

Provide state-by-state entries of a variety of helpful resources.
URL: www.newberry.org/nl/genealogy/AF-AMER-BIB/ Contents.html

▼ **Cyndi's List of Genealogy Sites on the Internet—African-American**

Links to sites for history, special collections, researchers, mailing lists, genealogical societies and groups
URL: www.cyndislist.com/african.htm

▼ **Family Search**

Church of the Jesus Christ of Latter-Day Saints has the premier genealogical collection, located in Salt Lake City, Utah. Beginners can visit the local Family History Center, known as stakes, for an introduction to the extensive source material.
URL: www.familysearch.org

▼ **HeritageQuest**

For state-by-state information on the availability of microfilm and sources
URL: www.HeritageQuest.com

▼ **Lest We Forget**

Emphasis on African American culture and preservation. Tells the stories of sacrifice and struggle.
URL: www.coax.net/people/lwf/

▼ **Roots Web**

General to specific information available
URL: www.rootsweb.com

▼ **USGEN Web Project**

Network of volunteers working to provide free access to records in every county and state
URL: www.usgenweb.org/

Archives

Debra L. Newman's *Black History: A Guide to Civilian Records in the National Archives* is an excellent resource. The National Archives and Regional Centers collection of documents, relating to African-American genealogy, include indices to bank deposit ledgers (1865-1874) and registers of signatures of depositors (1864-1874).

Noting the significance of these records, genealogist Sandra G. Craighead compiler of a *Bibliography of African American Genealogical Resources at Western Reserve Historical Society* said, "By revealing the surnames of brothers, sisters, and parents different from their own, depositor/ancestors help researchers gain new leads in finding a slave family before 1865."

These leads, she said, can prompt a search of wills, deeds, bills of sale under different slave owner surnames. She noted the scarcity of slave death records, allowing that some information would be almost impossible to come by, except for the bank registers.

Libraries

In America's heartland the Western Reserve Historical Society Library of Cleveland, Ohio, Allen County Public Library of Fort Wayne, Indiana, and Newberry Library of Chicago, Illinois are outstanding libraries with an emphasis upon genealogy. As far back as 1867, the Western Reserve Historical Society (WRHS) was one of the first institutions in America to formally express interest in genealogy.

Through the years, its library sphere of interest has extended from New England to Georgia and west to the Mississippi River, however microfilm resources available at the library extend far beyond Cuyahoga County borders. Although few institutions in the country have the complete United States federal population census schedule on microfilm, the decennial census, taken since 1790 is all available through 1930.

Valuable records at the WRHS Library include the following:
▼ Printed state census indexes through 1870,

▼ 1890 special census of Union veterans and their wives,

▼ Ohio mortality schedules listing deaths in 1850, 1860, and 1880,

▼ Cities directory for Cleveland,

▼ More than 3,000 manuscript Collections

▼ Union Catalog of American Genealogies,

▼ More than 60 microfilm rolls from the Ohio Surname Index to biographical material in various publication,

▼ More than 18,000 family histories.

WRHS research tools facilitate easy access to the library's numerous collections. Additionally researchers with a special interest in Cuyahogo County, Ohio, will find a treasure in the major African-American manuscript collections held by the Western Reserve Historical Society.

The African-American Archives focuses upon achievements going all the way back to Cleveland's founding in 1796. I was surprised to find a family member's name in Russell H. Davis' *Black Americans in Cleveland* published by the Associated Publishers in cooperation with the WRHS. I had not known that John Kellogg had been a city councilman.

With nearly sixty percent of its visitors registering as genealogists, the library's commitment to genealogy is steadily expanding. Fee-based library research services at over forty dollars per hour are available. As the recipient of the National Genealogical Society's Award of Merit for "being one of the finest genealogical libraries in the United States," the WRHS Library is prepared to assist.

The Library of Congress is the national library, located in Washington, D.C. It has copies of just about every book published. In addition the records of the National Association for the Advancement of Colored People, bound copies of *Flower of the Forest: Black Genealogical Journal* and much more are available there.

Sandra Lawson's *Generations Past: A Selected List of Sources for Afro-American Genealogical Research* highlight specific research available at the Library of Congress. Other notable libraries with special genealogical collections include the National Genealogical Society Library, Burton Historical Collection of the Detroit Public Library, Schomburg Collection of New York Public Library, and the Daughters of the American Revolution (DAR) Library.

County Historical Societies

I was contacted by the Anti-Discrimination Committee about setting up an exhibition in response to a KKK rally in my hometown. This was in the 1990s when I, and this view was shared by many, thought this KKK stuff was far gone. As if this were not enough to stop the Klan in their tracks, my work lead to me writing my book, *Freedom Road: Journey to Safe Harbor* (Closson Press 2005).

My work on this grass roots African-American history project has landed me an appearance on an Underground Railroad documentary, Safe Harbor, airing on National Public Television across the country. And what a surprise it was being named a recipient of the 2003 Afro-American Historical and Genealogical Society History Award.

What was gratifying that my people said that "their historian was to tell our story" and I was so honored to in the Mercer County Historical Society's 590-page book *Mercer County Pennsylvania Pictorial History 1800-2000* (Donning Company 2001), which carried my people's story. I earlier had been disappointed to see scant information about the African-American presence.

My people were no longer "invisible." My beautiful people's stories now were being told. The grass roots program indeed had achieved its goals, which included recognition of African-American contributions, increased self-awareness, and promotion of critical thinking. Comments at the exhibition opening held at the rotunda of the courthouse ranged from "Did you see that?" to "I didn't know slavery was ever here?"

Life Application

1. What relevancy, if any, does the "5" Core Values of Freed People have in present times?

2. Chart significant points on your personal journey to freedom.

3. Reflect upon the progressing, sometimes declining, degrees of freedom, compare and contrast the past and present times.

Endnotes

1   Adapted from the Aims of the American Society of Freedmen Descendants.

2   Kenneth H. Thomas Jr. "A Note on the Pitfalls of Black Genealogy: The Origins of Black Surnames," *Georgia Archive*, 6:1, spring 1978.

3   Carole Merritt, "Slave Family Records: an Abundance of Material," *Georgia Archive*, 6:1, spring

Chapter Eight
African Connections

"Where are your ancestors from in Africa?" Recent breakthroughs in DNA testing have helped in shedding light to a question that long had been unanswerable but for a select few. Just ask genealogist Karim Aldridge Rand. He now treasures his "Certificate of African Ancestry" that verifies his historical and cultural heritage.

You can look for fascinating results. There are people who have a fair complexion that have matches to a particular African ethnic group. Genetic research for the British Broadcasting Corporation's documentary Motherland revealed Y chromosome matches for one out of four African-Caribbean men from former British colonies with Europeans. So be prepared. DNA testing documents what we have known all along that there were some lusty white men siring slaves.

Rand was so grateful to find that his Y chromosome, which directly passed from father to son, matches that of the Makau people of Mozambique, East Africa. He proudly displays his package, which includes an explanation letter, the DNA sequence, a color coded map of Africa highlighting the region of African ancestry, and a copy of the interactive CD Encarta Africana. For years he had been looking to verify his strong sense of African heritage, passed down by word of mouth from generation to generation when he turned to DNA testing. Now he's got the proof.

African Ancestry
You too can have your proof. African Ancestry, a Washington-DC concern is a frontrunner in testing folks with African descent. African Ancestry, who provided Rand's testing, maintains that all DNA testing is kept confidential. African Ancestry has a large database of more than 10,000 genetic sequences from Africa, which allows for a

high accuracy rate in testing. Seven out of ten searches yield an exact match.

African Ancestry provides two types of testing, called the Matriclan Test and the Patriclan Test. Tracing your maternal ancestry can be performed by you, whether if you are male or female using the Matriclan Test. However to trace your paternal ancestry you must have a male, such as your father, brother, etc. to take the Patriclan Test. Both tests are taken through you rubbing the inside of your cheek with a cotton swab and returning through the mail.

Gina Paige, President
African Ancestry
5505 Connecticut Avenue, NW Suite 297
Washington, DC 20015
gpaige@africanancestry.com

or

info@africanancestry.com
Phone: (202) 723-0900
Fax: (202) 318-0742
Online ordering: www.africanancestry.com/ordermain.html

DNA testing comes at a price of between three hundred and four hundred dollars. Consider pooling resources for this heritage gift. DNA testing is available for Native American sequences and other populations. Megan Smolenyak's *Trace Your Roots with DNA: Using Your Genetic Tests to Explore Your Family Tree* (Rodale 2004) provides further discussion on this topic and a list of other DNA testing companies. Now you are at the threshold of Africa's door.

Planning Your African Journey of Self-discovery

Want to visit the land of our ancestors? My maiden transatlantic flight was a memorable experience. During my pilgrimage—Africa is popularly referred to as home by a generation of younger blacks—I was planning to reconnect to my African roots. The Atlantic was vast and impenetrable. She now blanketed the world. From back in my window seat I found, nestled in her arms, momentary solace.

Preparation is the key for anyone planning a journey to West Africa of self-discovery through heritage. Attorney James E. White's *Roots Recovered: The How To Guide for Tracing African-American and West Indian Roots Back to Africa and Going There* (Booklocker.com, Inc. 2004) will help you out with the preparation. Attorney White wisely counsels on how to travel on a budget and make a U.S. contact with someone from the countries you plan to visit.

Roots Recovered tells it like it is! Travel to West Africa can be thrilling. However, there are certain places where we need to be careful. Close attention needs to be paid to health issues, safety alerts and cautions for women. Particularly useful is the country-by-country at-a-glance chapters, which provide an overview of attractions, currency, language, and safety tips. Wish I would have had such a helpful book like this on my maiden trip to West Africa. I would recommend to anyone to read *Roots Recovered* before taking a trip to our ancestral home, Africa.

West Africa Travelogue

I captured a few vivid memories in my travelogue:
> *I was swept into a sea of blackness. The Air Afrique*
> *staff—all appeared Senegalese—were graceful and regal.*
> *I now, returned to Mother Africa for healing... When I found*
> *myself on the wrong side of corporate politics it took a toll.*
> *My feet first touched Africa's soil in Dakar, Senegal, where the*
> *climate was steamy hot. Water welling up against my kidney*
> *made matters all the more unbearable.*
> *I quickly located the men's room, following the arrow point-*
> *ing downstairs, my French being somewhat rusty. I ventured*
> *down the solitary cavernous passage to the dungeon, more a*
> *hole in the wall, I'd say. It wreaked of urine.*
> *I grasped my breath, darted in and out.*
> *I emerged only to find a squat attendant waiting for me,*

> *pointing to something; it was a worn 500 franc note.*
> *I didn't need no interpreter to see he wanted money.*
> *What a con, I thought. But, we were alone.*
> *I flipped a quarter on the table, and momentarily*
> *darted up the steps. Still, my host wasn't totally*
> *pleased as was evidenced by the harangue that followed me.*
> *—Is this Africa?" I wondered.*
> *Now Maulana Karenga has said that*
> *it may be harder being African than we think.*

***

Returning Home

Ghana was welcoming, breathtaking, full of grandeur and beauty, I thought. Now my first trip to Ghana was a highly-spirited one, retracing my ancestors' journey from freedom through the door of no return, the last stop in West Africa prior to embarking on slave ships. The Middle Passage—the voyage to the New World made by our ancestors and others leading to the expatriation of millions of Africans—secured our foothold in the Americas. I was committed to reaping every possible benefit.

Ghana, formerly known as the Gold Coast, has long been a land at the crossroads of Africa where there were many stark contrasts from the slave castles to the Ashanti palace. With plenty of pomp and ceremony our party was received at the Ashanti royal palace where the coos of peacocks filled the courtyard. In 1482, the Portuguese built Elmina Castle on the coast beginning the African slave trade.

I had high hopes of my journey to Ghana, though beyond the typical tourist traps I was unprepared on another level what I observed. I was shocked to find that some folk practice skin whitening. For more on skin whitening, check out N. Jamilya Chisholm's "Imitation of Life: Every Day Thousands of Ghanaians Risk Their Lives to Whiten Their Skin With American-Made Bleaching Creams. An African-American Writer Goes To the Capital City To Find Out Why" in *The Source* (October 2002). Due to so much of Ghana being left economically underdeveloped by the British a strong sense of "white is right" prevails. I realized that Africa was in need of healing.

Twelve African Traditions Alive in the Rural South

The Twelve African Traditions Alive in the Rural South was inspired by a delightful book Peter Sarpong's *Ghana in Retrospect: Some Aspects of Ghanaian Culture* (Ghana Publishing 1974), which I picked up as we browsed book stores in Ghana. It is generally agreed the tar-baby and tortoise and hare folk tales along with spirituals were transported from Africa. We see tangible evidence of African cultural patterns in Twelve African Traditions Alive in the Rural South, though the degree that African cultural patterns have survived in the United States is debatable. We honor our ancestors and reflect upon Twelve African Traditions Alive in the Rural South.

▼ God's omnipotent, omniscient and omnipresent

> The Adinkra symbol, "Gye Nyame," which is visible every-where in Ghana, is translated only God. It implies God is great and has power over everything and everyone. Akan of Ghana say sooner or later, and in one way or other, evil will follow wrong conduct . . . God does not show anger to those who unknowingly commit a wrong.[1]

Mr. Barksdale-Hall presents Oscar Larbi, librarian, with auto-graphed copy of People in Search of Opportunity for the Africana Collection at the George Padmore Research Library on African Affairs, Accra, Ghana.

▼ Virtue of Motherhood

The virtuous wife and mother was benevolent to her family and shared with strangers. Her praises forever were sung: Grandmother, the cooking pot that entertains strangers. The woman who gives to both mother and child.[2]

▼ Strong extended family ties

The extended family was a viable entity with corresponding responsibilities. Among the Akan, children were not permitted to enter into an adult conversation unless invited. Children were respectful, and willing to run errands.[3]

▼ Disciplined living

According to Eugene Genovese, "The African tradition . . . stressed hard work and condemned and derided laziness in any form."[4] To be abusive, talkative, drunk or excessively extravagant were dishonorable traits. Adultery and stealing were crimes against the community. Africa produced decorum and good manners. Genovese concluded, "The pity was that [the children of enslaved Africans] seem to no longer recognize how many such virtues their own forefathers had brought from Africa and contributed to the southern way of life—that they could not appreciate how great a contribution blacks had made to whites as well as vice versa." [5]

▼ Respect for Elders

An Akan proverb says there was an old man before a lord was born. Old age was venerated as the well of wisdom and experience, the portal to joining the revered ancestors. Respect for the chief, who was "over" the disposition of ancestral land, was rendered. Those who were in such high positions of authority were expected to exercise their power to punish discourteous and unwise followers. Conversely, failure to exercise power for correction undermined leadership and society.[6]

▼ Ancestral land in perpetuity

Ancestral land was to be preserved at all cost. In principle it is believed to be a future inheritance for the whole clan, including those yet born, to reap the benefit of. Everyone fundamentally was dependent upon the land. As the drum language of the Akan say, Earth, when I live I depend upon you, when I die, I depend upon you, Earth, you who eat carcasses.[7]

▼ Transmission of knowledge

Wisdom came through understanding symbols, signs and rhythm. Knowledge was transmitted through oral accounting, symbolic imagery and rhythm.[8]

▼ Significance of arts

African music and arts were integral to life. They are functional and belong to the community as a whole. Rhythmic clapping, ring-dancing and call and response were rooted in African traditions. African languages were complete with parables and double-entendres. Parables were part of everyday artistic expression and must be weighed for true meaning.[9]

▼ Sexual division of labor

Hunting, fishing, the tending of livestock exclusively were reserved to men, while women care for the home, cultivate a garden patch and sell chickens, eggs and other wares in the marketplace. Women bore bulky loads on their heads.[10]

▼ Value of interpersonal and spiritual relationships

The highest value was placed upon the person to person encounter. Spirituality was instrumental in shaping human existence. Mystical causes of sickness were sought out for spiritual meaning.[11]

▼ Rites of passage

There were traditions of the life cycle—birth, marriage and death.

Nicknames that described personal demeanor, physical attributes and family relationships were found in West Africa.[12]

Enslaved Africans normally did not view cousins as suitable marriage partners. The custom of marrying outside of the kin group likely was African derived.[13]

The decoration of burial sites with broken earthenware and other objects was found among the Bakongo of Angola and Akan of Ghana.[14]

▼ Sharing and honor

Among the Akan, generosity was a trademark. A stranger was given all necessary assistance, including free lodging and sometimes money. An Akan proverb says, the stranger does not sleep in the street. Any disregard for hospitality brought on disgrace. There was no death more awful than to die from any disease with a social stigma, called unclean. It was considered better to die in honor rather than to live in disgrace.[15]

Strengths and Weaknesses of Traditional Societies

We now move beyond glamorization of our African past to identify strengths and weaknesses of traditional African societies and point out the Ashanti participation in the slave trade. Weaknesses included the overemphasis on spiritual belief systems to the detriment of technological systems coupled with tribalism, as evidenced in ethnic tensions, which played a role in the slave trade. Hotel Rwanda gives some exposure to ethnic tensions, which incidentally further were exploited by European colonialists. So we're not going to belabor present times, though our restoring work calls upon a critical eye for analysis of both past and present events.

In the wake of Ghana's political independence Chinua Achebe wrote his now classic novel, Things Fall Apart *(1958). He sought to provide an African perspective to view cataclysmic changes in leadership brought on due to the African encounter with Europe.* Things Fall Apart *is recommended reading for those with an interest in this pivotal period in African history. He portrayed the values of pre-colonial Igbo society and culture that were both stabilizing and destabilizing. Because he established the existence of "history, religion, civilization" and leadership in pre-colonial Africa and vindicated Africa' glorious past, he challenged Europe's justification for colonialism in Africa (Ravenscroft, 1986, p. 7).*

Ethnic Tensions

How do you bring together people of various ethnic backgrounds for the common good? In the aftermath of the Nigerian Civil War, then celebrated novelist Chinua Achebe showed an interest in issues related to tribalism and social responsibility. The Civil War was a direct response to rising ethnic tensions. Given that Nigeria's boundaries were established without consideration of ethnicity, government leaders face a major challenge.

Central to the conflict in contemporary Nigeria has been social tensions between the Igbo and other ethnic groups. Dominant ethnic groups in Nigeria include the Igbo, Yoruba, Fulani and Hausa and at one time or another in history were hostile to one another.

*The War left an enduring mark on the writer, as reflected by a more pronounced interest in political matters. Achebe, an Igbo chief, served in the secessionist government and personally witnessed the death of many kinsmen. Achebe's literary works—*Things Fall Apart, No Longer at Ease *and* Anthills on the Savannah*—examined the effect of social change upon leadership in Africa, a continent of extraordinary diversity. Achebe offered open discussion among the stakeholders as a solution to build bridges to unity across tribalism and other social divisions, though he refrained from inviting peasants to the table, reflecting his own personal bias as an intellectual, the exclusion of poor people from dialogue being short-sighted. His vision pointed toward a greater agreement for Africa's response to future challenges.*

Strengths of Traditional Igbo Society

▼ *Strong family ties*

▼ *Religion stressed the importance of elders; each person had a personal chi that helped in having children and during times of sickness*

▼ *Loyalty to clan members*

▼ *Court system promoted order. Clan members desired peer approval and avoided taking any action that might bring shame on the family thereby causing ancestors to bring evil down upon them.*

▼ *Men and women had respective roles in the social order*

▼ *Respect for the ancestors and elders*

▼ *Self-esteem and pride in their heritage*

▼ *Agricultural system provided a supply of food and shelter.*

▼ *High value on human life. Laws protected against killing any of their own people.*

▼ *Basic medicinal training*

▼ *Established economy with shells and yams as currency*

Weaknesses of Pre-Colonial Igbo Society

▼ *Illiteracy. The Igbos really became excited about learning to read and write*

▼ *Sacrificing of human lives caused separation among the people*

▼ *Lack of a centralized government with no hereditary rulers or elected chief*

▼ *Religious beliefs caused doubt about the white man's power*

▼ *Next generation's faith in customs was weak*

▼ *Outcastes were abandoned and not cared for*

Collective Healing

African scholars recognize Elmina Castle as being the earliest known European structure in the tropics. There, enslaved Africans were held in damp cramped oppressive dungeons prior to the Middle Passage. Royal families in England, Spain, Portugal, and France, as well as the leadership of the Ashanti, Benin, and Congo, who supported the slave trade by selling Africans to Europeans in exchange for merchandise, share a major burden for this horrific episode.

I heard a public apology from our African brothers for their role in the slave trade. Yes, I did. I heard it with my very own ears. Well, it was so healing. I captured a mental snapshot of the moment, as it related to our collective healing.

The most provocative session for the Association for the Study of Classical African Civilization (ASCAC) Conference held in July 1996, that I have attended, has been the program of Firhanka International, being translated "when leaving home no good-byes were said."

Several chieftains along with Nation of Islam representatives presented the community land development project—30,000 acres in the Eastern Region were available—along with plans for repatriation of Trans-Atlantic-slave-trade-descendants. The chieftains begged forgiveness for their ancestors' role in selling us into slavery.

African leaders have begun the process to usher in our collective healing, though the mainstream media has taken little note. The New Millennium was hailed with the President of the Republic of Benin, the Honorable Malhieu Kerekou at a reconciliation conference offering a public apology for their role in the slave trade. He said, "We owe to our selves never to forget these absent ones standing among us who did not die their own deaths. We must acknowledge and share responsibility in the humiliations." *Washington Afro-American* reporter LaWanda Johnson's feature, "Benin seeks forgiveness for role in slavery," was carried in *The Final Call* (October 8, 2002).

On our side of the Atlantic the Million Man March signaled a turning back to families. Just leaf through the *Million Man March/Day of Absence: A Commemorative Anthology* (Third World Press and University of Sankore Press 1996). A season of collective healing has come. In 1997 we named our newborn son Imanuel-Tiefing, which means "God is with the African Man" in hope of this great day.

Jah Kente International, Inc.

Back home, participation in the healing process through my role as president JAH KENTE INTERNATIONAL, INC. with a mission to nourish and promote the cultural spirit of Africans in the Diaspora has been rewarding. The public entity was granted nonprofit 501(c)(3) status by the United States Internal Revenue Service (IRS) on March 8, 2000.

We have held lively performances on the grounds of the Frederick Douglass home in Washington, DC. We presently look forward to co-sponsorship of a clinic in Mali. For more information, visit the Jah Kente International, Inc. Website www.JahKente.org.

Jah Kente International, Inc. programming offerings include:
1. The Tiefing Collection—an exhibition/curatorial presentation featuring selected articles of a private collection of African and South Pacific artifacts acquired by the curator, Rufus T. Stevenson, during his work and travels in these areas of the world.

2. "Redemption Ritual"—a literary (choreopoetic) presentation of classical African American poems by famous African-American poets, including Countee Cullen, Langston Hughes, Robert Hayden, Margaret Walker, Richard Wright, Sterling Allen Brown and James Weldon Johnson. Produced by Rufus T. Stevenson, Co-Founder of Jah Kente International.

3. "Slave Genealogy"—a genealogical presentation demonstrating how you too may research your family's history, and gain insight, health and strength remembering SANKOFA—an old African Adinkara symbol meaning "look to the past and fetch it." Presented by Roland Barksdale-Hall, Co-Founder/ President of Jah Kente International.

****

West Africa Travelogue

In Accra, Ghana I scheduled a noon luncheon appointment with Kofi Kwakyei. Six hours later, he arrived; few things run on time given travel conditions. Kofi was married to Theresa, a Newnan (Georgia) girl; marriage joined together the American Waters, Stevensons and Ghanaian Kwakyeis.

Kofi walked right up to me in the Novotel lobby. It was our first time meeting in person. He walked right up and said.

—I'd know you were a Stevenson anywhere in the world.

***

Today, Kofi blessed me "Barksdale, you are more African than the African."

Now, life had gone full circle. I had retrieved what (global connections) our ancestors' lost.

Rufus T. Stevenson (far left), descendant of slave ancestor Sam Stevenson and co-founding executive vice president, along with the author, co-founding president. Both officers of JAH Kente International.

Through my mind a favorite passage from Ayi Kwei Armah's *Two Thousand Seasons* flashed. "Remembrance has not escaped us... [W]e, fraction that crossed mountains, journeyed through forests, shook off destruction only to meet worse destruction, we, people of the fertile time before these schisms, we, life's people, people of the way, trapped now in our smallest self, that is our vocation: to find our larger, our healing self, we the black people..."

Family clan celebrates common origins at the Stevenson/Waters Family Reunion, Newnan, Georgia

Life Applications

1. How do you bring together people of various ethnic backgrounds for the common good in your backyard? What about gay and straight? What about Anglos and Latinos? What about Ethiopians and African-Americans? What about Muslim and Christians?

2. Mona, a contemporary African-American sister in Halie Gerima's classic film *Sankofa* says, "*Stop! Don't you recognize me? I'm not an African—I'm an American!*" What relevancy, if any, does ethnicity, race or religion have in today's global marketplace? What about in your hometown?

3. Which of the Twelve African Traditions Alive in the Rural South are evident in your family group? What is their particular significance?

4. What are some barriers to unity in your community? How might you overcome them? Who are the stakeholders in the problem? How might you extend your self to bridge the door to open discussion about the problem? What common ground do you share with other stakeholders? Why is it in your best interest to work together? What potential problems might arise through your efforts to bring the community together?

5. How can we better affirm spiritual beliefs along with staying abreast of latest advancements in science and technology?

Endnotes

1   Alfred Kofi Quarcoo, The Language of Adinkra Symbols (Legon, Ghana: Sebewie Ventures, 1994), p. 1; Peter Sarpong, Ghana In Retrospect: Some Aspects of Ghanaian Culture (Accra-Tema, Ghana: Ghana Publishing, 1974), p. 12.

2   Peter Sarpong, Ghana In Retrospect: Some Aspects of Ghanaian Culture (Accra-Tema, Ghana: Ghana Publishing, 1974), p. 69.

3   Ebenezer Mireku, Which Way Ghana? Restoring Hope and Confidence in the Ghanaian (Accra, Ghana: Asuso Peabo Ltd, 1991), p. 61; Peter Sarpong, Ghana In Retrospect: Some Aspects of Ghanaian Culture (Accra-Tema, Ghana: Ghana Publishing, 1974), pp. 70, 97.

4   Eugene D. Genovese, Roll, Jordan, Roll (New York, Vintage Books, 1976), p. 115

5   Peter Sarpong, Ghana In Retrospect: Some Aspects of Ghanaian Culture (Accra-Tema, Ghana: Ghana Publishing, 1974), pp. 35-6.

6   Peter Sarpong, Ghana In Retrospect: Some Aspects of Ghanaian Culture (Accra-Tema, Ghana: Ghana Publishing, 1974), p. 65.

7   Peter Sarpong, Ghana In Retrospect: Some Aspects of Ghanaian Culture (Accra-Tema, Ghana: Ghana Publishing, 1974), pp. 116-17.

8   Adapted from The Philosophical Aspects of Cultural Difference, Developed by Edwin J. Nichols, 1523 Underwood St., N.W., Washington, D.C. 20012.

9   A.A. Agordoh, Studies In African Music (Accra, Ghana, New Age Publication, 1994), pp. 28-57.

10 Peter Sarpong, Ghana In Retrospect: Some Aspects of Ghanaian Culture (Accra-Tema, Ghana: Ghana Publishing, 1974), p. 66; Jacqueline Jones, Labor of Love, Labor of Sorrow (New York: Vintage, 1985), p. 39.

11 Peter Sarpong, Ghana In Retrospect: Some Aspects of Ghanaian Culture (Accra-Tema, Ghana: Ghana Publishing, 1974), p. 25; Adapted from The Philosophical Aspects of Cultural Difference, Developed by Edwin J. Nichols, 1523 Underwood St., N.W., Washington, D.C. 20012.

12 Carole Merritt, Homecoming, African-American Family History in Georgia (Atlanta: African-American family History Association, 1982), pp. 21-22.

13 Carole Merritt, Homecoming, African-American Family History in Georgia (Atlanta: African-American family History Association, 1982), p. 68.

14 Eugene D. Genovese, Roll, Jordan, Roll (New York, Vintage Books, 1976), pp. 200-11; Carole Merritt, Homecoming, African-American Family History in Georgia (Atlanta: African-American family History Association, 1982), p. 86.

15 Peter Sarpong, Ghana In Retrospect: Some Aspects of Ghanaian Culture (Accra-Tema, Ghana: Ghana Publishing, 1974), pp. 27, 66.

Chapter Nine
Health Matters

Mint Americana

Raccoon faced engines draws Americana;
Inside separate but equal etch slumber:
Black face porters mime errand boys;
Belly-heavy conductors haunt corridors.

At another time, the hmmmmmmm...
Of the Dixie Flyer carried;
Coffee people, shoebox lunches;
Chickens (both alive and fried);

Miles mo' on elastic bumble seats
Packed in Jim Crow cars, bushes...
Blot fo' Birmingham gals' sleep.
Tain't easy, movin' toilets, you know.

Good health covers your physical, mental, emotional, spiritual, and social well being. You can begin to explore health matters in asking a few simple questions. What diseases run in your family? Who has been affected with what? Where did they live? What was their age at the beginning of the disease? What happened? Jot down any major health matters with parents, grandparents, aunt, uncles, brothers, sisters, and first cousins. To rap about health matters can help to save your life.

Breast Cancer, Lightning Does Strike Twice

During the sixties my mother fought a personal battle. She, having located a lump in her breast consented to visit a doctor. When the doctor diagnosed her as having a benign tumor and told her she need not worry as long as it did not bother her, my mother let out a sigh of relief.

My mother prudently sought professional care. However, she erred in not following up when she began to experience discomfort and notice changes in her body. "I shortly forgot about the incident. I had you and three other children to raise," she would later recall.

But cancer research has revealed some startling facts that my mother and other women like her have not always had the benefit of knowing. According to the National Cancer Institute in a recent publication titled, Spread the Word about Cancer: A Guide for Black Americans, "Breast cancer is the second leading cause of cancer death for African American women. Between 1973 and 1992, breast cancer in African American women ages 50 and older increased more than 38 percent, and the death rate for this increased 25 percent."

The National Surgical Adjuvant Breast and Bowel Project (NSABP) list several characteristics that are risk factors for breast cancer:

▼ Over 50 years of age—in general, as age increase, the risk does,

▼ A family history of breast cancer (mother, sister or daughter),

▼ Never bearing children or having the first child after the age of 30,

▼ A history of benign breast disease that required biopsies,

▼ Early menstruation (before age 12) or late menopause (after age 50), and

▼ Being more than 40 percent overweight.

As the health literature points out, this does not mean that other, low-risk women will not get the disease, nor does it mean that the high-risk will definitely get cancer.

Recently, The American Cancer Society (ACS) Breast Cancer Risk Factor Study revealed that individuals with a family history of breast cancer and history of benign breast disease were found to have the highest relative risk.[1] According to Herbert Seidman, Assistant Vice President of Epidemiology and Statistics of the American Cancer

Society, "Because these factors are those that are most genetically determined and, thus, not subject to preventive measures, these women should indeed receive a great deal of monitoring."[2]

What my mother failed to recognize was that developing a benign tumor of the breast and having a family medical history of breast cancer placed her in a high-risk category. Individuals like her and my aunt, who are in the high risk group, traditionally have been more susceptible to breast cancer.

As a child, I can remember my mother talking about Aunt May, and the long suffering from an accident. During the 1940s, as Aunt May was helping her husband dig their basement, she was struck in the breast with a pick. As many blacks during that time did not obtain proper medical care, Aunt May never complained as her health rapidly deteriorated.

Similarly, my mother suffered, enduring years of surgery, chemotherapy, and loss of hair. This was primarily due to her misjudgment of the condition. When she noticed changes in her body, my mother should have consulted her physician. Early detection of her breast cancer likely would have saved her life. "Her cancer, however, was too far gone, when she began treatments," doctors explained.

According to Dr. Helen E. Ownby in an issue of the Journal of the National Cancer Institute, "Recent reports indicate that breast cancer in blacks is not only detected at a later stage ... than in whites, but show a consistently lower survival rate for all cases and within each stage. These observations point to the necessity for an increased emphasis on early detection of breast cancer in black women."[3]

While significantly high percentages of our population are being affected by disease, we too frequently remain the last to learn of its consequences. Research unfortunately reveals too many black women, like my mother, wait later than whites for diagnosis and treatment.

In the aftermath of mother's death I decided to uncover Aunt May's story and shed light on our family's medical history. I began by obtaining the booklet titled Where to Write for Vital Records: Births, deaths, Marriages, and Divorces, from the U.S. Government Printing Office, in Washington, D.C., and proceeded to request the death record of Mary Steverson McClendon from the Department of Vital Records. To request a death record, you need to know your family member's name, state or county of death, and approximate year of death.

Comparison of the death records of Aunt May and my mother led to conclude, lightning can strike in the same spot within a family. The condition leading to Aunt May's death was carcinoma of the right breast, with an interval of four years between the onset of cancer and her death. In this case, my evidence supports the findings of earlier researchers, that a direct link exists between heredity and susceptibility to breast cancer.

Dr. Florence Demenias, an epidemiologist, has begun a family study on breast cancer in the African American community—the first systematically performed study of this kind. Her study is aimed at detecting specific genetic effects among all factors causing the disease. In her recent article in Genetic Epidemiology, Dr. Demenias stresses, "the need to design family studies in order to permit some progress in the understanding of complex diseases, like breast cancer."[4] She adds, "For all cancers, choices of lifestyles can affect your risks. People should decrease the fat in their diet and eat more fresh fruits and vegetables."

Although current health information reveals "breast cancer is not caused by bumping, bruising, or caressing the breast,"[5] today we need to be health savvy.

At age 74, my aunt has become an example of what I consider a health-savvy individual. When the doctors diagnosed the lump in my aunt's breast as benign, at her request they removed it. My aunt continues to have regular checkups, aggressively seeks out health information, and consults with professionals. In major decisions related to her health, she asks for a second professional opinion. To eat right and exercise has improved her outcome. My aunt recognizes that nobody can take care of her body like she can.

Through effective education and the study of your family's medical history, you can facilitate the early detection of breast cancer. With the support of the American Cancer Society and researchers at the National Cancer Institute, we can further improve our understanding of breast cancer and once again join in the celebration of good health.

Racial and Ethnic Disparities in Health

The National Medical Association (NMA), NAACP and the U.S. Department of Health and Human Services have launched initiatives to eliminate racial and ethnic disparities in health. The focus is on disparities in six key areas:

▼ Breast and cervical cancer screening and management,
▼ Infant mortality,
▼ Cardiovascular disease,
▼ Diabetes,
▼ HIV/AIDS infection rates,
▼ Immunization rates.

Experts have begun looking at other factors, which have been ignored, including smoking, obesity, and mental illness. African-American men tend to be more affected by nutrition-related diseases and need to increase their daily portions of fruits and vegetables.

Family Health History

Have any of your family members (including parents, grandparents, aunts, uncles, brothers, sisters, and first cousins) had the following?

Ill Health	Who?	Age the illness began
Alcohol addiction	_____	_____
Bleeding diseases	_____	_____
Cancer (what type?)	_____	_____
Depression	_____	_____
Diabetes	_____	_____
Drug addiction	_____	_____
Heart disease	_____	_____
High blood pressure	_____	_____
High cholesterol	_____	_____
Osteoporosis	_____	_____
Sickle Cell Anemia	_____	_____
Strokes	_____	_____
Other	_____	_____

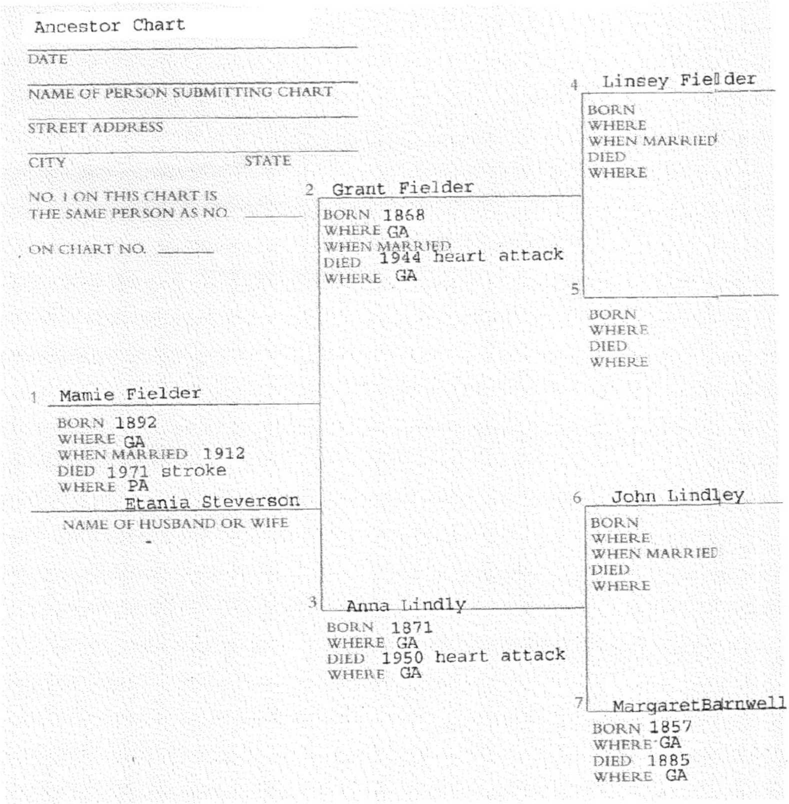

Ancestor Chart

DATE

NAME OF PERSON SUBMITTING CHART

STREET ADDRESS

CITY   STATE

NO. 1 ON THIS CHART IS
THE SAME PERSON AS NO. _____

ON CHART NO. _____

4 Linsey Fielder

BORN
WHERE
WHEN MARRIED
DIED
WHERE

2 Grant Fielder

BORN 1868
WHERE GA
WHEN MARRIED
DIED 1944 heart attack
WHERE GA

5

BORN
WHERE
DIED
WHERE

1 Mamie Fielder

BORN 1892
WHERE GA
WHEN MARRIED 1912
DIED 1971 stroke
WHERE PA

Etania Steverson

NAME OF HUSBAND OR WIFE

6 John Lindley

BORN
WHERE
WHEN MARRIED
DIED
WHERE

3 Anna Lindly

BORN 1871
WHERE GA
DIED 1950 heart attack
WHERE GA

7 MargaretBarnwell

BORN 1857
WHERE GA
DIED 1885
WHERE GA

Figure 3

Popular Sites

African-Americans and Diabetes
www.diabetes.org/communityprograms-and-localevents/
africanamericans.jsp

Closing the Health Gap
www.omhrc.gov/healthgap/index.htm

Diabetes Statistics for African-Americans
www.diabetes.org/diabetes-statistics/african-americans.jsp

Mobilizing African American Communities to Address Disparities in Cardiovascular Health
www.nhlbi.nih.gov/health/prof/heart/other/balt_rpt.htm

National Cancer Institute:
www.nci.nih.gov/

National Medical Association
www.nmanet.org

Office of Minority Health
www.omhrc.gov

The National Medical Association (NMA) launched the W. Montague Cobb/NMA Health Policy Institute (Cobb Institute) to serves as a resource on health matters of ethnic and racial groups and look for solutions that will enhance the quality of health care for all Americans. Dr. W. Montague Cobb was a trailblazer in the struggle for hospital integration and among the National Association for the Advancement of Colored People (NAACP) leadership. At Howard University I served as Coordinator of Black Health History and was liaison to biomedical research centers in the Caribbean and West Africa. I consulted with Dr. W. Montague Cobb to put together an exhibit which was a salute to African-American history in the health sciences. The goal of the exhibit was to depict the earliest involvement of Africans in the health sciences, and some present-day spin-offs of their discoveries. It highlighted the contributions on Imhotep , who in Egypt in 3000 B.C. designed the world's largest first large man-made stone structure, practiced medicine, and wrote the monumental Ebers papyrus; and Hatsheput a queen of Egypt, who in 1500 B.C. practiced the arts of healing. On display were the first Proceedings of the Imhotep National Conference on Hospital Integration (March 8-9, 1957). Sponsors of the Conference included the National Medical Association, National Association for the Advancement of Colored People (NAACP), and the Medico-Chirurgical Society of the District of Columbia. Dr. W. Montague Cobb and Dr. John A. Kenney, Jr., with the support of numerous Howard University graduates, led the push for hospital integration.

Charting Your Family's Health

You can use a simple tool, called the genogram, to chart your family's health.

The genogram can be used to show the physical, mental, emotional, spiritual, and social patterns of your family. You can begin to understand your family better as you construct your genogram. The genogram can be viewed as an expanded ancestor chart, though charting your ancestor chart can make available valuable information. For example, charting the ancestor chart for my Grandmother Mamie Fielder Steverson revealed the same cause of death for both her parents. I had noted on the ancestor chart that my Fielder Great-Grandparents died of heart attacks, which likely was contributed to by their poor diets. However, I did not dismiss that my Grandmother Steverson's cause of death listed as stroke also was cardiovascular related. To view your genogram provides a concise method to uncover patterns beyond the obvious which are emerging in your family system over generations.

The Stevenson Family Genogram shows physical, mental, emotional, spiritual, and social patterns in my family. The genogram can show names, places of birth, marriage, and death, though you initially can benefit in charting your genogram without this information. As earlier mentioned, you can request death records of ancestors, if you are unaware of the cause of death. Given how families did not discuss health matters in the past, it probably is a good

Stevenson Family Genogram

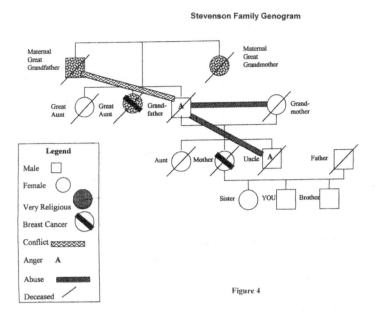

Figure 4

idea in any case to request the death record to verify the cause of death. In the Stevenson Family Genogram the reoccurrence of breast cancer over several generations is evident. You can look up medical terminology in a medical or nursing dictionary. You can consult your physician about the cause of death. It is important that you note the age at beginning and duration of the illness.

My Stevenson Great-Grandparents, considered sanctified, were very religious and conservative. They did not condone drinking or smoking. Meanwhile my Grandfather Stevenson, considered a pug, gambled and made homemade wine in his basement. The difference in lifestyles led to a cool distance between my Stevenson Grandfather and his father. The conflict between father and son did not produce any verbal displays or showing out rather it was evident to all that the older man did not condone his son's behavior. The son's removal of his immediate family from the sanctified church where his father, sister, and her husband worshipped signaled a cooling of the relationship.

I now was better able to understand through charting the Stevenson Family Genogram where change was needed. My Stevenson grandfather had high hopes. His name Etania, which meant wealthy and successful, reflected his ambitions, though he was not to achieve his goal. He had numerous setbacks due to poor personal choices coupled with racism. He coped with poverty and life's disappointment through drinking and violence. He did not develop true relationships with his wife and children, but he attempted to dominate and control through physical abuse, manipulation, and coercion. His children, who found nurturing relationships in the women in their lives, described their household as a reign of terror.

A son, who became a classic cool cat, adapted these coping strategies and leashed out at the world until he realized a change in his behavior was necessary. For more about being cool and macho, read Richard Majors' *Cool Pose: The Dilemmas of Black Manhood in America* (Touchstone 1992). However, the lack of true relationship between family members was passed from generation to generation.

Creating Your Genogram

As you begin to gain awareness about the intergenerational patterns in your family, you then can consider what might be done to change your behavior so that you might not be overcome by the same situation. Get a big sheet of clipboard paper. Arrive with symbols that represent death, divorce, marriage, conflict, and stable relations. Males typically are represented by a box and the females by a circle. To represent a marriage or other male/female relationship draw a line between the partners. Custom has it that the male appears on the left and female to the right. You can refer to the key or legend in the Stevenson Family Genogram.

Charting your genogram you can examine the following:

▼ Naming practices—jot down nicknames of family members, common adjectives (both positive and negative) used in discussion of ancestor. What roles did family members play?

▼ Defining spaces—How was personal treated? What were relationships like between parents and child? Were closed doors respected? What about other relationships in the immediate family? What about other relationships in the extended family? What about the important relationship between grandparents and grandchildren?

▼ Bonding—How did family members relate to one another? Were they clinging? Or was there a distance? How did they view non family members, boyfriends or girlfriends who wanted to enter their circle? How did the family respond in a crisis?

▼ Quality of family life—How would you characterize the structure of the family? Who was in charge? Who participated in the rule making? Who was the enforcer? Who was the nurturer? How would you characterize the household? Was it rigid or disorganized? Or maybe there was give and take, which is a healthier pattern?

▼ Rules—What were the understood, yet sometimes unstated, rules about the family? What were the core values and beliefs?

There is nothing wrong with seeking help to look at the past. If it be a trusted elder, spiritual counselor, psychologist, physician, or support group, you can seek out the support that you need. This process initially can be challenging for some, and a bit painful for others, though you need to honestly look for situations that produced lasting affects, both positive and negative, in your family. To pinpoint where, when, and sometimes how or why strengths or weaknesses came to exist in the past can help you in the present, remembering lightning does strike twice.

Life Applications

1. Complete your family health history? What runs in your family? What constructive steps can you take to live a long and prosperous life?

2. Create your family genogram. What patterns emerge?

3. Where is change needed in your lifestyle?

Endnotes

1   Relative risk was defined as the ratio of the age-standardized incidence rate in a given group, divided by the incidence among the group having no risk factors.

2   A Different Perspective on Breast Cancer Risk Factors. American Cancer Society, 1983.

3   H.E. Ownby et al., Genetic Epidemiology. 75, 225 (1988).

4   F. Demenias et al., Genetic Epidemiology. 5, 225 (1988).

5   One in 10 women will develop Breast Cancer, Howard University Cancer Center.

Chapter Ten
Healing Through Storytelling

Maybe you are related to a famous person? Genealogist Robert H. Williams found he is. He only wishes that he earlier had been aware of his connection to Banneker.

"I always liked history, but it was not one of my best subjects in Grammar School," he recalls.

How differently things might have been if he would have known of his connection to Banneker? He reflects upon the glaring absence of all but a few African-Americans from the American history books in school. Still, he is hardly able to believe that he is related to Benjamin Banneker. The discovery makes him and a host of relatives feel proud.

What Shall We Tell Our Children

It is important that we encourage our children. I am reminded of a favorite story of mine, which I love to tell. The following tale was inspired by Margo Humphrey's delightful book, *The River That Gave Gifts: An Afro American Story* (Children's Book Press 1978). A delighted audience applauded my presentation of "What Shall We Tell Our Children," at the Oakland Public Library in California.

> *Lydia lived on an island down by the riverside. She did not live in a wood house. She did not live in a brick house. She lived in a thatched roof hut.*

> *Lydia had a special friend. Her name was Ola. Ola was like everyone's grandma. Ola would gather together all the children from up the river and down the river and serve coconut and roasted yams.*

It so happened one day Ola's eyes began to dim. And the children wanted to celebrate the life of the elder.

Now Lydia thought she had ordinary hands. She could not make anything. She sat under the coconut tree down by the riverside. Some say she was asleep. Others say she was awake. But the river began to talk to her.

"Take me in your hands. Take me in your hands."

She grabbed a gourd and ran and scooped up some water. As she ran the living water spilled on mother earth. Yet there remained some.

When she reached Ola's hut, she greeted the elders. She then poured the water into her hands, and she rubbed her hands together and took her hands and opened them. Out of her hands came red, yellow, orange, blue, indigo and violet. Light filled the room.

Now Ola could see, and everyone realized that Lydia did not have ordinary hands, but she had the hands to break the coconut and serve roasted yam. For she had special hands. And in those hands flowed the gift of life.

A Sense of Somebodiness

Our children need a sense of somebodiness. Giving them a connectedness to the past can help, which comes through storytelling. Granted, everybody might not be related to Benjamin Banneker or a famous personality. Still, everybody has a community history to explore.

For several years I actively participated in a school-community partnership that my local genealogy group spearheaded with the Martin Luther King Elementary School in Pittsburgh. I and a colleague, Ida Mary Lewis, focused our energies upon developing a stellar voluntary enrichment program for fifth graders, known as "Self-Discovery Through Heritage."

We became keenly aware that our children need hope of a brighter future, as we exposed the youth to what an heirloom was. We were rapping about what heirlooms in the family were, when it suddenly dawned on me some of the youth were separated from their families. So we explored how if they created a wonderful piece of artwork and managed to care and preserve it until some day when they had grand-children, the treasure the artwork would be to their families.

"What gift from the heart would you like to create for your grand-children in the future?" I asked. The children pondered. The children thought about the question, I had asked. The positive image of them, creating strong, healthy families, was empowering. I witnessed a positive change was occurring.

Self-Discovery Through Heritage

Our introduction to the urban classroom was memorable. Youth appeared like they were not there. Some had their heads down. Others got up and sharpened their pencils while I was talking. Yet we remember catching a flicker in some of their eyes. The teeny flicker of hope drew me back again and again. Our work was like reviving a drowning victim.

We rapped about the dilapidated New Granada Theater, a familiar landmark in Pittsburgh's Hill District. I researched the landmark and presented my preliminary findings, which included a photo of the cornerstone dated 1927 along with a March 12, 1927 front page story, "K. of P.'s To Erect $300,000 Temple" from the files of *The Pittsburgh Courier*. The building had been designed by L.A.S. Bellin-ger, an African-American architect, built at a major cost by the Knights of Pythias during the 1920s, and viewed with racial pride.

Our beautiful African-American children came alive, as we talked about African-American Underground Railroad Operators and the genealogy of buildings in our community. . The children were no longer desensitized to the past. So on a personal level each was better equipped to answer. "Who am I?"

Our wonderful children had been revived. They were curious, alert, and responsive again. They were excited when I ran into them around town. They were running up to me and introducing me to their family members. They had begun a journey of "Self-Discovery through Heritage." Please let us give our children a gift of self-discovery through heritage. Our children need to know that they come from a striving African-American community.

The Pittsburgh Public Schools' Reporter (vol. 15 no. 7) praised the school-community partnership. "Fifth graders at King, taught by Margaret Lewis, are proud of their multicultural project. In partnership with Lewis, Roland Barksdale-Hall, executive director, Western Pennsylvania African-American Historical and Genealogical Society, is teaching students to do genealogical research.

Students also are learning the African-American history of their school community, located on Pittsburgh's North Side. Barksdale-Hall shares his expertise—and the magic of historical research—through games, activities, slides, and video presentations." I soon was asked to share my successful ideas for multicultural programming to the Balch Institute's Philadelphia Pittsburgh Teacher Partnership.

Our children will treasure a gift of heritage forever. Don't be surprised if they show their appreciation. Finally, the children at the Martin Luther King Elementary School nominated me to be a KDKA Television New Pittsburgh Hero for my community service. And to my surprise, I was selected. A television spot about the "Self-Discovery Through Heritage" program aired throughout the city. How was that for a show of appreciation?

Truth Telling

The nation's oldest African American religious organization the African Methodist Episcopal Church recently made history elected Rev. Vashti M. McKenzie, it's first woman bishop in the church's first 218 years. The jubilant anointed woman of God reaffirmed the vitality of strong sturdy bridges of sisterhood throughout Black church history.

Positive images of the African-American mother pretty much have survived slavery up until recent times, though the image of the African-American male was less than favorable. The emasculation of the African-American male—be it through castration or weakening of spirit or other means—has historical roots in an economic system. The system devised to perpetuate slavery and three hundred plus years of unequal status, which fractured and fragmented African-American family life. The Million Man March publicly made atonement for the absence of the African-American male in families.

"I stand on the shoulders of the unordained women who served without appointment or affirmation." Bishop-elect McKenzie with tears in her eyes thanked the Saints in the house. "I stand tonight on the shoulders of the local women who could not be itinerants, but nevertheless, they loved God and they served wherever they were." (Carter, 2000, p. 8).

The nods of women's heads in affirmation to a story that I tell about the sacrifice of African-American women in rural settlements in the South signify an Amen corner.

Silver Spoons, Sweet Water and Sisterhood

Samantha was sweet as sugar. Guess, that's why everybody called her, Saint. Saint was born with a silver spoon in her mouth, some might say. When Luther Jackson's intent to court her—one of the Lester gals—became known, she accepted with just one minor stipulation. I'll stay with you just so long as we has milk, butter on the table, and food to eat, Saint said.

Luther was nine years her senior and agreed. Proved himself a mighty good provider. Not only did he provide for her but for heaps of family, friends, and travelers.

Saint was the best cook in the world! She made some of the biggest fluffiest biscuits that you ever tasted in your life. Oh it was great to go there and eat! Well, travelers never got enough. Her custards, overflowing with butter, just kept the folks coming back for more. Oh it was just like dying and going to heaven!

"Well, it's raining we can't go home," colored travelers said.

Sure enough, folks came up with all kinds of excuses why they weren't leaving today. On the farm the work of a God-fearing woman was never done. Saint tended a large vegetable patch. Dried peaches and apples. Canned all kinds of berries, peaches, pears, and apples.

Now, Saint was a good Christian. She never cooked on Sunday. She was Methodist. All the food preparation was done the night before. She carried wonderful spreads for lunchtime to church.

Sweetwater Methodist Church was a special kind of place. Some said the church was named after an old Cherokee chief buried somewhere nearby. Others recounted the story of dem Hebrew chillen. After being led out of captivity in Egyptland they came to a place where the water was bitter. They tasted that water and grumbled against their leader. Folks called the place, Marah. Now, that meant bitter.

Fittingly, old Moses had done everything he could, to try and please them. Now, old Moses, he fussed some, cried, and kicked a whole lot before throwing in the towel. He was dejected, at a loss for words. Well, sometimes when you reach your wits end, you open up to trying something a little different. That's right where old Moses was. He had reached the end of his rope. Serving others can do that.

Old Moses saw the need to confess up to his weakness. That took eating a little humble pie. All the same, that's how he got his breakthrough. Why that was all it took for him to receive what to do. God is an ever-present help in the time of trouble. It was at Marah that Moses let go and got his release, dem bitter waters being made sweet.

So every Sunday there was a redemption ritual for colored country women. At church Saint and many weary sharecropper's wives in the company of one another got their release from the day-to-day drudgery of waiting hand-and-foot on others. It did the church women's hearts so good to see one another make it down the aisle.

Right after morning service let out, the sisters—church women called one another sisters in recognition of their close bonds—gathered outdoors on the church grounds. Sisters set out on the picnic table beautiful spreads, everybody just helping themselves to whatever was there. Under the cover of a great, big old oak tree whatever spiritual and emotional release remained to be got, the sisters got off of one another's shoulders. Strong bonds of sisterhood were sturdy bridges to wholeness. It took coming together, crying on one another's shoulders, hugging and sharing intimacy for invoking country colored women's commitment to living. God is my witness; Saint lived for Sweetwater Church!

Saint now had got her bounce back. She was ready to face the world again. It was a good thing too, because half of it was waiting for her at her home. She was busy waiting on a crowd of colored preachers, presiding elders, and her husband, who all had their legs stuck under her dinner table on her day of rest. And what a talking and eating they done! Now, it was her husband's time of renewal.

Into the evening she waited upon them. Afterwards she cleaned up. She washed the Sunday plates—tin plates were used during the week—and utensils and put them away before dragging to bed. Her body was tired, but her soul refreshed.

Collective Healing

How can stories be used to bring to bear understanding of the past and collective healing? I puzzled with this question. My book, *Healing is the Children's Bread: Complete with the Holistic Health Guide*, self-publishing in 1999, undertook to reconcile our past and bring collective healing. I collected the not so glamorous stories of dispossessed African-Americans from various walks of life. The book broke new ground, as evidenced in the table of contents.

"What was my inspiration in writing *Healing is the Children's Bread, Complete with the Holistic Guide*?" I frequently am asked. Over fifteen years ago now, I nearly was electrocuted in a freak accident at work in Washington, D.C. You see the accident left me crippled, in constant pain and unable to work.

We went six months without receiving a payment from workers comp, all the while expecting a baby. It was an all-time-low. So it was in chaos the inspiration to write a book about pain and suffering first came, you might say.

What was my biggest challenge in putting my book together? For the book to be genuine I had to locate real people who were willing to lay bare their soul. Still somehow it happened. People came forth and shared powerful healing testimonies about their struggles with past demons, be it slating the dragon of self-worthlessness or doing the right thing at the right time. The book's study guide hopefully will point you in the direction to get the healing process underway.

TABLE OF CONTENTS

Cultural Connectedness

From Broken Vessels to Re-creation

Seven Lessons for Life

The Voices of a Thousand Children Speak about Life

My Journey to Freedom

Single Parenting

The Great Pumpkin

Crossing the Color Line

Great-Great-Grandmother Rillis, My Namesake

Black Entrepreneurs Still Going Strong

Bread of Praise

The Level of God-Rule Living

Setting at Liberty Those in Bonds

Bloods and the Hood

Mommy Dearest: Lessons in Forgiving

A True King and Queen

A Sense of 'Somebodiness'

Doing the Right Thing at the Right Time

The Aurora Reading Club

Reflections of the Elder, Baba Kofi Ojisé

The First African American Graduate of the University of Pittsburgh

Slaying the Dragon of Self-worthlessness

For Life, Love Is

Mending Broken Promises

When God Knocks at your Door

Urban Renewal Ain't Got to Spell 'Black Church Removal'

Breast Cancer: Lightning Does Strike Twice

From Situational Leadership to SuperLeadership

French Fries and Faith

Complete Guide to Holistic Health

Resource Guide

Choose Life Today, and Live

If there's one lesson to remember after reading *Healing is the Children's Bread, Complete with the Holistic Guide*, I'd say, "We can choose life today, and live."

"We've ignored violence (in America), especially when it takes place among the poor and minorities. As a nation, wee have not taken violence seriously enough, thus allowing it to flourish." Former United States Surgeon General, David Thatcher, now director of the National Center for Primary Care at Morehouse School of Medicine in Atlanta says.

Warm tears swelled up at the retelling of "Bloods and The Hood." I once again was reminded of my Godson's bullet-riddled body. The story of him being shot a block from his home bears out, in recent times there is an alarming escalation in violence. The choice to live or die, to taste new wine or to sup the dregs of bitterness may be a personal choice. Yet the fallout from the many wrong choices touches us all. Consequently, the need for collective healing cries out.

Story Telling

By virtue of our strong African-American oral tradition story telling offers a great avenue for reaching the entire community. Telling your healing story begins with a story map.

Story Map

Title_____

Author_____

Setting (When and Where)_____

Characters_____

Opening Sentence_____

Idea One_____

Idea Two_____

Idea Three_____

Closing Sentence_____

Just try and stick to the same opener and closer. Then build upon your three main ideas. Allow freedom for variation in the telling of your story. With the story map you can craft interesting family stories.

Planning is the key to successful story telling. The presenter must read the selected story over and over again to gain familiarity and can be dressed to draw attention. Kente cloth, head scarf or some other accent are wonderful accents. Command of the voice can be used to draw the audience to their feet.

Story Planner

Title_____

Presenter_____

Props_____

Idea One, Time Set Aside, Style of Delivery_____

Idea Two, Time Set Aside, Style of Delivery_____

Idea Three, Time Set Aside, Style of Delivery_____

Moral of the Story _____

Learning Outcome _____

Give careful thought to what props to use. Puppets also are good aides. I picked up my puppets at Parent teacher Outlets. I have a menagerie of stuffed animals, which I use for animal folktales. I picked up my stuffed rabbit after Easter at a bargain. Bells, shakerais, drums, and the belephone, which is a xylophone-like wooden instrument, I also have used. A cask iron skillet and wooden spoon can draw attention.

What life lesson do you expect someone to leave with? The moral of the story deserves careful thought and consideration. Sometimes, the moral of the story is spelled out. Other times it can be left for the listener to piece together. Yet, it pays to ask a few follow-up questions to see if the listeners got what the life application to the story is. Whatever your expected life application is, we refer to as the learning outcome.

Today, stories are told through the blues, rap, poetry, personal accounts, African-American history, heroes and sheroes, fables and folktales. *Poetry from the Master, The Pioneers: An Introduction to*

African-American Poets, edited by Wade Hudson, (Just Us Books 2003), for example, provides a selection of classics in poetry. You can get other ideas for storytelling from books at your local library.

Write It Down

I was fortunate to be on a panel, "Getting Our Voices Heard: Black Librarians and Publishing," at Clark Atlanta University in Georgia at a time when the historic library school was looking closure in the eye. I tried to be upbeat and shared five motivational points of publishing.

▼ Passion

Set a goal to pursue your passion. I undertook writing a health piece about breast cancer just because I had a passion there. Due to my mother's breast cancer late detection she had a premature death. I was fired up enough to make a difference. My people have gained a reputation as an oral people, without realizing that we, too, are gifted in other ways and have a story to tell.

▼ Perspective

You can begin with market research, by reading what others have written on the topic. Read *Savoy, Essence, Ebony* and *Crisis Magazine*. Check out *Black Issues Book Review* to see what others are writing about.

Now ask yourself some questions. If you wrote your story, who would you want to read it? Who else possibly would benefit from it?

▼ Perseverance

Be organized. I would be a rich man for how many times I've heard tips for getting organized at writer's conferences. Request Writer's Guidelines from magazines.

What to do while you wait for the guidelines to arrive? Most folks were not born writers but worked hard at it. Review some basic principles of writing found in *The Elements of*

Style by Strunk and White. You can find editors to help smooth out rough edges. Just make sure that you got something to say.

▼ Promotion

What spin-offs do you foresee from the project? So many times folks write a family book and don't take the time to figure how to market it. Check out *Writer's Digest* and Takesha D. Powell's *The African-American Writer's Guide to Successful Self-Publishing* (Amber Books 2004) for sound marketing ideas. You have got to arrive with ideas to get your material out there.

▼ Presentation

Bring your own flare to the presentation. Folks like to hear a passage from your book. You can practice reading out loud. Let who you are come out!

Spirit of Sankofa

"I wish to repeat that we need to write our own history. The hand that holds the quill controls history. Too often we, as African-Americans, have been left out of the history books. It is time for us to sit down and write about our own history," author Charles Blockson charges.

Nobody can tell your story for you. It is so important to realize that you have a treasure trove of family stories and life experience to share. In the slave quarters stories were used so children could get some understanding. "Minding your own business and leaving others to paddle their own boats" was one such value. What healing stories have you let go of? Child, go back and fetch those things.

Reading List

Carter, A. Y. (July 19, 2000). AME church makes history, elects first woman bishop. *Buckeye Review*, p. 8.

Life Application

1. Compare and contrast the leadership roles played by African-American men and women in the family and the community in present times?

2. What pearls of wisdom can yo*u recall that* family members shared?

3. How can you pass on pearls of wisdom to future generations?

4. What passion do you have? How might you share your passion with others?

Chapter Eleven

Twelve Keys to Health, Wealth, and Success

Key One: Practice conversion

An African-American model of conversion offers insight for us getting back on a healing path. Conversion in its simplest element means the process of an ongoing life change, moving from one state of being to another higher. We tend to talk about conversion in the context of from profane to spiritual, though it speaks to life change in general. Stories of great spiritual men and women, including Mohandas Gandhi, Martin Luther King, Jr., Mother Theresa, and Malcolm X, are commonly known. The process of conversion needs to be worked out, as we live out our lives.

Let's now take the time to explore the principle of conversion from a bigger picture. Here are just a few simple examples.

- ▼ Complacent to compassion
- ▼ Unforgiving to merciful
- ▼ Isolation to community
- ▼ Unhealthy to healthy
- ▼ Suspicion to trust
- ▼ Nonethical to ethical
- ▼ Close-minded to open-minded
- ▼ Pride to humility
- ▼ Ignorance to wisdom
- ▼ Inconsiderate to considerate
- ▼ Anger energy to loving action
- ▼ Chaos to peace
- ▼ Spendthrift to prudent
- ▼ Dishonest to honest

▼ Unrestraint to self-control
▼ Immaturity to maturity

Try and look at each new life challenge as stirring us from out of our comfort zone, poking us to soar higher, higher and higher. In our hectic world we need to take time out to focus upon personal growth and development.

Key Two: Rap with our elders

We all every so often need to hear what life is about. I applaud the commitment of Master teacher Haki R. Madhubuti, who is hosting forums for young brothers across the country, though we desperately need more rap sessions with elders in our community. It is unfortunate that so many of our youth are unaware of the wonderful contribution of dynamic African-American men and women to the world, as we know it.

In a western Pennsylvania milltown an African-American community based program, called Conversations with Elders holds hope, as elders dispense pearls of wisdom. Otey, 80 of Sharon, Pennsylvania, challenged young people to make the right choice at the right time and to know they are somebody.

Children sat at the feet of the elders and learned about what it was to overcome the spitefulness of separate but equal school and adversity with dignity.

"Don't let anyone… make you thing that they are smarter than you." Elbert Otey, counseled. "Only you can make yourself dumb."

If we cannot connect with elders in our local community or at a rap session, then read one of the following books. A must read the sage Madhubuti's book, *Tough Notes: A Healing Call for Creating Exceptional Black Men* (Third World Press 2002) provides brothers wise counsel and food for thought. Dorothy Height, who actively has been engaged in progressive action throughout the Civil Rights Era and admirably served at the helm of the National Council of Negro

Women, has a compelling book *Open Wide the Freedom Gates: A Memoir* (Public Affairs 2003).

Key Three: Put our dollars to work

In recent times I learned that one spelling of my Grandfather Steverson's first name Etania was an Indian word, which meant "wealthy." It blew my socks off that my Stevenson Great Grandparents had such high hopes. What was more amazing that they succeeded in reaching their goal. They possessed great wealth, which included eighty acres, a two-story house and six rental units, where the tenant farmers lived who worked their land.

The secret of our ancestors' wealth was that they reinvested their little money into more lucrative ventures that brought in a higher return. Great Grandfather Wilson Stevenson, who saved an amazing fifty cents of every dollar he made, and a generation of former slaves practiced good business sense.

We have got to put our dollars to work in this economy if we are to succeed like our ancestors. There exist stock dividend reinvestment programs through the National Association of Investors Corporation, which we can participate with a small investment. We can organize investment clubs. For other strategies to put our dollars to work, read, Melvin B. Miller's *How To Get Rich When You Ain't Got Nothing: The African-American Guide to Gaining and Building Wealth* (Amber Books 2002), Dorothy Pitman Hughes' *Wake Up and Smell the Dollars! Whose Inner City is This Anyway!* (Amber Books 2000), Paula McCoy Pinderhughes' How to Be an Entrepreneur and Keep Your Sanity (Amber Books 2004), and Larrette Kyle DeBose's *The African-American Guide to Real Estate Investing* (Amber Books 2004).

Born of slave parents Archie Stevenson and Harriet Allen, Samuel and Wilson Stevenson represent just two of a slave family of fourteen children. They were slaves on a Stephenson plantation in Newnan, Georgia. In slavery's aftermath there was chaos. No matter, a generation of former slaves purposed in his heart to leave a financial legacy.

> *If you undertake a Life History interview with a parent, Grandparent or other relative, you will never regret it.*
> —WILLIAM FLETCHER
> Author, *Recording Your Family History*

When Mary Steven Waters was not quite fifteen, she married Jim Stevenson and moved onto the Stevenson homestead in Evergreen, Georgia. At that time a small community, Evergreen was a few miles outside of Newnan. She shared the following recollections about the rural farm economy.

Memories of Pa Sam Stevenson

For many years Mary Waters Stevenson and her husband faithfully lived and worked beside his parents, Samuel and Lorena Stevenson. She came to respectfully know them simply as "Pa Sam" and "Ma Reena."

Pa Sam was proud and industrious. Except for the way he pronounced a couple of words, to know him you wouldn't have guessed he was a former slave. With high cheekbones and an acquiline nose, Pa Sam was a tall slender man. He could have passed for an Indian if it hadn't been for his light brown complexion and fluffy soft hair.

He might not have known how to read or write, but Pa Sam was pretty swift and knew how to mind his own business. Like most people, he began as a sharecropper, yet he worked his way up to become an independent landowner—he came to own plenty of land. Back in 1885, he purchased his first parcel of land: 40 acres from M.N. Calley. Over a twenty-year period, he managed to acquire almost 200 acres.

Stud Service for Bulls

Pa Sam made money a variety of ways. He took a huge bull and opened up a stud service. If your heifer cow was goin' low, you would bring her over to our place.

"Can my cow get along with yours?" neighbors customarily asked.

"Yes!" Pa Sam would say, and when the neighbor's heifer had her calf, Pa Sam received a dollar from him.

When a heifer gets with calf, you keep milking her. About a month before the calf was due, Pa Sam quit milking the heifer, and once the calf was born, he would resume his daily milking of the cow. For the first two or three weeks after the calf was born, we'd feed that milk to the hogs.

Stud Service for Hogs

Pa Sam ran a stud service for hogs, too. Only with hogs, when the sow had a litter, the neighbor provided you with one piglet from the litter. Pa Sam was shrewd. Before he had a male pig, he simply let the lady hogs run free.

Now if John over yonder had a gentleman hog and his hog got together with Pa Sam's sow and they had a litter, Pa'd say, "I don't know whose hog it was and I don't have to give you any of my litter." He just let nature take its course. No way in this world he'd have known where the piglets came from.

He sold charcoal, chickens, turkeys, guineas, ribbon cane syrup, sorghum syrup, peanuts, sweet peas, crowder peas, and pigs. Within six weeks after an old sow would come in, he'd sell those piglets. His note was as good as gold.

Key Four: Bond to healthy communities that;

1. Continue to safeguard freedom for yourself as well as others

Freedom was earned at a great personal cost and needs to be preserved through taking personal responsibility for our actions while maintaining a healthy compassion for others, wherever attainment of progress has been reached there was human struggle. Across the front cover of the spring 1992 *Alleghenian*, Frederick Douglass' clarion call to personal responsibility—if there is no struggle, there is no progress—was carried as a sound reminder: Personal freedom comes at a cost and we can ill afford to take it for granted.

2. Accept others

Healthy, growing communities make room for people from different backgrounds. Elks accepted people into membership regardless of family background, socioeconomic status, or moral character; a policy that fostered a healthy community spirit and contributed to its popularity among southern migrants. Organized in 1914, and remaining intact in an era marked by disunity, Twin City Elks Lodge of Farrell, Pennsylvania's membership (which included unskilled southern workers as well as the elite of the community and everyone in between) peaked at over seven hundred, and all managed to coexist peacefully—a remarkable circumstance, offering a model for framing social progress. So it is that God looks beyond our faults to love us and we are to pass the love on.

3. Join together for the common good

The Brothers and Sisters of Love rallied around Brother James A. It was a powerful vision of a place of corporate worship, set in Pennsylvania's picturesque wooded, rolling terrain where there were beautiful buildings, senior Saints Home, and cemetery in 1917. The word of the Lord was precious back in those days. With excitement people from

Sharon and Pittsburgh mortgaged their homes and pooled resources to purchase a tract of land, 127 acres. After completing a day of hard work Sharon steel workers came together to build what has become known as Zion's Hill, working until it was dark; on Saturday they were joined by the brothers and sisters from the Pittsburgh church.

Today, crowds of joyful worshippers continue making the annual pilgrimage to Zion's Hill. The proud heritage, that we are recipients, is thanks to a tiny band of believers, "the Brothers and Sisters of Love," who purposed in their hearts to please God and through sincere acts of faith initiated, unbeknownst to them, what was to be a national reformation movement. As Voice of Calvary, Jackson, Mississippi, Bread for the World, Silver Spring, Maryland, and Sojourners, Washington, D.C. attest, there continues to be hope for transformational change within communities that pray.

Key Five: Take responsibility for our communities and ourselves

In recent times, there is a heightening edge to public conversations and an alarming escalation in violence. The role of the media in promoting machismo and militaristic types notwithstanding, we must navigate the choppy waters to safe ports where healthy dialogue is encouraged, nourished and sustained, thereby fostering better understanding. As a dynamic, cross-cultural activity, I organized an open forum concerning rap music.

We must take responsibility for ourselves and establish personal and communal boundaries. A deep gratitude is owed the African-American woman. We need to say "no" to negative lyrics that bash sisters and besmirch their character. We understand that economic pressures propel some rappers to make use of whatever means available to escape poverty, though we need not condone the spread of harmful materials in our community. We need strategies to resist the flow of harmful materials in our community.

Street culture need not become equated with our rich African-American culture. A conscious-raising community-based program, entitled "Hip Hop: the African Roots of Contemporary Black Music" that I organized, sparked a wide-ranging intergenerational discourse about language, role models and the state of the African-American community. Dialogue in and of itself is not expected to restore civility to America, though it is a first step along the road toward taking back our community.

Key Six: Vote in local, state, and national elections.

Voting can make the key difference. More minorities—particularly African Americans, Hispanics, Native Americans, economically disadvantaged whites, and the elderly—are needed as elected officials.

The global community has been exposed to women in new roles as engineers, astronauts, and heads of state. This generation witnessed the rise to power of former Pakistani Prime Minister Benazir Bhuto and former Phillipine President Corazon Aquino, both coming from renowned political families. Former prime minister of Great Britain Margaret Thatcher took a humble background as a grocer's daughter and established a ground swell of popular support. Stellar character, one of Thatcher's natural assets, distinguished her from traditional aristocratic cronies. These leaders struggled against overwhelming odds to establish a global presence.

During his first presidential campaign Bill Clinton reflected savvy in addressing significant women's issues. Among the concerns are employment opportunities, education, legal rights and health care. The voices of women responded playing a pivotal role in the presidential election, with an aftershock being sent to Republicans—women stand ready to vote for candidates who support specific issues. Former House Speaker Newt Gingrich correspondingly moved to close the gender gap that showed more women voting Democratic.

Women are increasingly entering the political arena. The new generation of female lawmaker appears not quick to bow to stereotype, sexism or intimidation. Then, why should they? While nine of 10 working women are of child-bearing age and the majority are planning to have a child some time along their careers, many of today's

THE WHITE HOUSE
WASHINGTON

March 15, 1999

Mr. Roland C. Barksdale-Hall
939 Baldwin Avenue
Sharon, Pennsylvania 16146

Dear Roland:

Thank you very much for your message of support and for the
material you enclosed.

As we prepare to meet the challenges of the 21st century, it
is important to me that I know the thoughts and experiences of
people who care about the future of America and our world. I am
confident that, working together, we can protect our shared
values and meet our common challenges.

I'm glad you took the time to write, and I welcome your
involvement.

Sincerely,

Bill Clinton

women—unlike their counterparts in the 1950s—will remain in the workforce, with economic issues playing a major role in the decision.

U.S. Rep. Maxine Waters of Los Angeles, by pulling off an upset for the coveted Congressional Black Caucus' chair, served notice that underestimating the new generation of women's political savvy can be costly, some tough days are still ahead. As more women and other minorities enter the political arena, refreshing, the change promises to be. To vote restores empowerment in the community (Barksdale-Hall, More women needed as elected officials, 1997, p. A-6).

Key Seven: Read more, increasing our cultural awareness.

In recent times, Oprah Winfrey has been credited with doing much to promote social responsibility through reading. She continues a tradition rooted in the African American culture, extending back over a century. The 100th anniversary celebration of the Aurora Reading Club, hailed by the New Pittsburgh Courier as "one of the most dignified and elegant affairs," held at the grand University Club in Pittsburgh's cultural district was a milestone in women's history, old Pittsburgh and Black culture (Farrish, 1994, p. B-1). The founding of the Aurora Reading Club (1894) coincided with the emergence of a vibrant women's movement across the country in the 1890s.

Despite limited economic opportunity beyond domestic at the turn of the century, Pittsburghers adopted proactive strategies to advancement, their interests both as women and people of color being explored through a program of "systematic study" (Page et al., 1994). From the outset the Aurora women exhibited not only a passing interest in the vital issues of the day but a commitment to social responsibility, which continues today. The legacy included a strong belief in family values and the passionate pursuit of knowledge through purposeful reading. Aurora was an allusion to the Roman goddess of the dawn, "symbolizing the dawning of a new era with hope for a new day at the turn of the twentieth century."

The African American women's club movement was not a mere imitation of Caucasian pursuits but an opportunity for naturally curious women of color to explore their interests. In synchronization with the national women's club movement, Aurora provided a vehicle for Victorian-era women of color to spread their moral influence while through a study of current events making inroads in expanding upon a mutual goal: the pursuit of freedom and equal opportunity. According to Paula Giddings, "between 1892 and 1894, [African American women's] clubs proliferated throughout the country, from Omaha to Pittsburgh, Rhode Island to New Orleans, Denver to

Jefferson City" (Giddings, 1984, p. 83). The women were confronted not only with race matters but gender obligations. Aware of changing times, the women sought through reading to move beyond their personal concerns and addressed the vital interests of the day.

In the late twentieth century, African American librarians are not only promoting reading but in the vanguard in the struggle for social equity. The respect that E.J. Josey, the first elected African American male president of American Library Association, has earned among the entire community is due in part to his unwavering commitment to the principle of social responsibility.

Kathleen E. Bethel, African American studies librarian, has exhibited a similar career pattern. She has served as an observer of elections in South Africa. Their commitment to literacy and community leadership have appeared seamless. Reading changes lives. For a good selection of cultural titles worthy of reading, see the *African American Literature: A Guide to Reading Interest,* edited by Alma Dawson and Connie Van Fleet (Libraries Unlimited 2004).

Key Eight: Know our history

History is a positive force that will counter the needless destruction of young, impressionable minds. Every child, particularly females, African Americans, Hispanics, Native Americans, and disadvantaged whites, could benefit from learning about their history because of its many redeeming values. Children are especially vulnerable to subliminal messages and, therefore, are in special need of developing positive self-images.

Executive Director of the Ohio Rites of Passage Network, Paul Hill, Jr. warns communities that if they will not counter the negative bombardment with good news, what might happen. "Lacking historical consciousness and social conscience, the African American male youth represent a great irony: they are the new warriors, only they ravage the people instead of the people's enemies." Yet, the picture doesn't have to appear so bleak.

What can we do to nurture growth and positive development?

1. Tell positive stories about our ancestors and their struggle for freedom and expanded opportunity. Join a genealogical society and learn more about tracing your family history (Barksdale-Hall, How to nurture positive self-images, 1989, p. 5).

2. Read cultural and historical magazines. Either subscribe to at least one or check them out at your local public library. Then share what you learned. To borrow from a popular saying made prevalent on America's historic black college campuses: each one reach one, each one teach one.

3. Take cultural excursions. Positive exposure to cultural celebrations, historic sites and cultural centers go a long way in driving home a point.

4. Uncover the hidden heritage of minorities in your own backyard. Worthwhile local projects include walking tours, exhibits and slide shows. Some are oral history projects, cultural bingo games and collages of local freedom fighters. Others are cultural murals, essay contests and read aloud programs. There are preservation projects, stories of laborers and migrants, and cultural calendars. The list is endless.

5. Take stock of the material heritage. Memorabilia are valuable items made by, written by or about, or depicting the image of a particular group of people. Jeanette Carson owner of Black Ethnic Collectibles, based in Hyattsville, Maryland, is the largest promoter of African-American memorabilia and art in the country and recognizes the underlying economic factors associated with collecting ethnic material culture, saying "many people are beginning to understand the historical importance of African American memorabilia while others are seeing it as an unique and profitable investment."

Take Stock of Our Heritage

Minority cultural institutions must be more vigilant. The events surrounding the Alex Haley Auction reveal the African American community's vulnerability when it comes to taking stock of its material culture. After the staff of the National Afro-American Museum and Cultural Center in Wilberforce, Ohio, heard of the impending auction, they had only two weeks to solicit donations that allowed them to purchase papers, photographs and other memorabilia.

Yet, with a small amount of funds the National Afro-American Museum and Cultural Center purchased sufficient items to develop a modest exhibit, which documents the life of Alex Haley. John E. Fleming, director of the National Afro-American Museum and Cultural center, however, conceded, "We, as a people, had again allowed our cultural heritage to pass out of our hands and to be dispersed beyond the control of our institutions."

> *Enlightened leadership is service not selfishness*
> *—Lao-tzu, author of Tao Te Ching* [1]

What will happen to valuable ethnic collections in the future? It is clear that without vigilance, further expansion of the lucrative material culture market will continue. The disposition of ethnic materials is a community matter, with particular significance to the African American community.

There are some things that we can do. On the local level we can press for greater representation of our ethnic community on board of directors of museums and historical societies. We can support a Native American, Hispanic, African American or women's museum in our area. We can press for greater ethnic representation on city and state advisory boards.

Across the country, concerned citizens need to take stock of their multiethnic material heritage, remembering if we don't know the past, we won't be prepared to meet our future (Barksdale-Hall, Historian says it's time to take stock of African American material heritage, p. 8).

Key Nine: Celebrate life's passages and instill positive values

While African Americans cannot recreate Africa here in the United States, they can retrieve what is good from the past. Judging by the amount of ritualistic activity in African culture, the transition from youth to adult ranks as one of life's most significant events; it is paralleled only by birth, marriage, and death. This delicate life passage logically bears attention on this side of the Atlantic.

An African-oriented view of socialization recognizes life's passages. Among the Masai of East Africa mid-life is a time of reflection when men stand at the threshold of a passage. Junior elders not only lay down their weapons but rely on diplomacy. An African process for ritualization of social relationships can be adapted to an American context.

Rites-of-Passage

The elders of Sankofa Institute of Pittsburgh are committed to the African proverb—it takes a village to raise a child. Sankofa is a Ghanaian word literally translated as "return and pick it up." According to Alfred Kofi Quarcoo, we must pick up the gems from the past (1972, P. 17). The Pittsburgh Institute established in 1992 is implementing Rites-of-Passage Rituals for youth, both male (simba or young lion) and female (malaika or little angel) grades 8-12. Requirements for initiation consist of completion of readings on black history; 20 hours of community service; mastery and internalization of the Nguzo Saba (seven principles of Kwanzaa); learning and internalizing of the Black National Anthem and Black Family Pledge.

During a recent ceremony held at a church, initiates made public pledges to: continue their education; use their education towards maintenance, development and the future of African Americans; and serve as role models in their communities. Only youth completing high school and requirements mandated by Sankofa Institute and its Council of are eligible for initiation. The Institute recently instituted a number of activities including after-school mentoring, historical reading, drumming and dance, and fencing along with numerous outdoor recreational activities.

The Passage Model for African-Centered Development of African American Youth, designed by Anthony Mitchell, a Mwalimu (teacher) of Sankofa Institue, includes: manhood training, physical fitness, and survival training. Some components are sex education, health maintenance, and financial management. Others are racial awareness, spiritual enrichment, and educational reinforcement.

Discussions of values and what it means to be a responsible African American adult are par for the course, remembering there is no such thing as either a free lunch or value-free world. Other folks are always imparting values to our children, intentionally or unintentionally. It's high time that we spell ours out to our own children, plain and simple.

The exact number of male Rites-of-Passage initiatives across the country remains unknown. Inspired by the 21st Century Commission of African American Males, the Black Collegian undertook a national search for "programs geared toward saving the African American male." Provided the grassroots nature of most Rites of Passage initiatives, the survey was unable to provide an accurate representation of their numbers.

But what is certain that from Boston to San Diego, an African stream of consciousness is sweeping the nation, altering perceptions and attitudes, and revitalizing the black family. The wisdom of African and African American ancestors has been chosen as a guidepost (Barksdale-Hall, The Passage, 1993, p. 4).

Key Ten: Build bridges to confidence, unity, and restoration

Eliciting potential critical thinking holds promise for building bridges to confidence, unity while preparing tomorrow's leaders to meet the formidable challenges ahead. South Africa provides a model for framing progress. Out of travail, a stronger, more inclusive nation was born on May 10, 1994. The jubilant President Nelson Mandela celebrated the triumph of justice, ushering restoration into a once conflict-driven land. Mandela's powerful words of reconciliation were balm to the hearts of both black and white.

The newfound statesman spoke, "The time for healing of the wounds has come. The moment to bridge the chasms that divide us has come. The time to rebuild is upon us."

It was a mere six years earlier, during the height of the struggle between the apartheid South African regime and the church, Archbishop Desmond Tutu delivered to the white South African nobility a prophetic message: "You have already loss... We are inviting you to come and join the winning side." Crystal-clear insight, truth-telling and the loving power that bonds humanity together are rays of hope along an arduous journey.

Key Eleven: Excel in what we do

According to James Kouzes, "leaders must keep hope alive. They must strengthen our belief that life's struggle will produce a more promising tomorrow." Hampton University under the transformational leadership of President William Harvey has become a model of excellence in the African American community. There, a harmonic blend of the traditional and contemporary continue to exist.

The balance of academic integrity, character development and assessment (outcomes measurement) is producing gifted young people, who are prepared to stand tall in today's competitive job market. Moreover, Hampton University's strong alumni-base has remained committed through giving.

Today, the Afro-American Historical and Genealogical Society (AAHGS) is a national organization with more than twenty chapters across the country. The phenomenal growth of AAHGS is due in part to the progressive vision of one transformational leader, Sylvia Cooke Martin. A decade ago, then the newly-elected AAHGS president, Sylvia realized that a window of opportunity existed for the formation of chapters and spearheaded a major membership campaign. What was the cost of skyrocketing growth? In her inaugural address Sylvia candidly shared, "First, you can expect commitment. I have a tendency to work on projects as if they were my last venture... Expect commitment and intensity—they are my nature..." (Martin, 1988, p. 3).

Through the promotion of excellence she not only achieved notable change, but significantly contributed to the organization's national reputation (Barksdale-Hall, The Afro-American Historical and Genealogical Society..., 1996, p. 2). Subsequently, Sylvia's enthusiasm inspired others. Just as important, the motivational leader delivered what she promised. In recent times, people are longing for credible leadership who will practice what they preach.

Secondly, she called together stakeholders (old members, new members, and nonmembers) whom she deemed to be creative, outspoken and committed, and early sought their involvement.

Finally, she was instrumental in recruiting younger people—I was thankful to be one of those that she recruited—and took a healthy interest in mentoring them for future leadership.

Key Twelve: Take a calculated risk, pursue our passion, and birth a vision

To pursue your passion will furnish the drive to carry a work-in-progress to completion. History shows that recognition sometimes can be slow in coming. Until recently there has been little acknowledgement of African American inventors, despite their significant contributions to the growth of this country (Chappell, 1997, p. 40; Barksdale-Hall, African American inventive genius, 1995, p. 3). Similarly, painters, scientists and community organizers must have the stick-to-itiveness to see a vision birthed.

The reach of helping hands have extended into kitchens, neighborhoods and hamlets where we live and work. At the turn of the century Mary McLeod Bethune with just a pipe-dream and one dollar and fifty cents in her pocket took a calculated risk. She succeeded in building the forerunner of Bethune-Cookeman College and a community hospital in Florida. As she traveled through the valley of dry bones, her passion for serving humanity kept the fire kindled in her soul. We too must reach deep in our spiritual reservoir to birth a fresh, revitalizing vision of our community.

> *If your son laughs when you scold him, you ought to cry,*
> *for you have lost him; if he cries, you may laugh,*
> *for you have a worthy heir.*
> — Senegalese proverb

Life Applications

1. View the Twelve Keys to Health, Wealth, and Success as a roadmap, guiding us to new places. Rank the twelve in order of importance to your life. What is the most important key? Why?

2. It is vital that we maintain hope in the face of adversity, as we continue to make strides toward realization of The Twelve Keys to Health, Wealth, and Success.

Problem Solving Guide

We are including a handy guide for problem solving, just in case if we run into any obstacles on the way to meeting our life goals. If we do not succeed once, rethink the situation and try again.

Step 1. Identify what the problem is in three sentences or less.

_____

_____

_____

Step 2. What events occurred that you to conclude there is a problem?

_____

_____

_____

Step 3. Make timeline. Show the growth of the problem. Where did the problem begin? How did the problem develop?

_____

_____

_____

Step 4. Who are the other people interested in the problem? What is their story as it relates to the problem? Are they interested in a solution to the problem? Why do they need a solution?

_____

_____

_____

Step 5. What are the known facts?
—Include factors such as people, resources, costs, and constraints

_____

_____

_____

Step 6. What is unclear, but it would be helpful to know? It might be attitudes, relationships, and hidden costs.

_____

_____

_____

Step 7. Identify the best solution as you presently see it. What is the likelihood of it working?

_____

_____

_____

Step. 8 Draft an outline of a plan for implementation. Look at the consequences of your plan. Identify similar situations in our past and the outcomes. Note, what additional facts, if available, would cause us to change our mind.

_____

_____

_____

Step. 9 Implement the plan. Here's to Health, Wealth, and Success.

_____

_____

_____

Step. 10 If the plan doesn't work the first time, reevaluate steps 1-6 and develop a new plan in steps 7, 8 & 9.

_____

_____

_____

NOTES

1. John Heider, *The Tao of Leadership*. (Atlanta, GA: Humanics New Age, 1985), p. 13.

2. The *Problem Solving Guide* adapted from Charles H. Kepner and Benjamin Tregoe, *The New Rational Manager*. (Princeton, Princeton Research Press, 1981), discussions and handouts from *Decision Making and Problem Solving for Leaders* (Spring 2000) by Quinn Leoni.

Chapter Twelve

Restoring the Family

How do you carry on after the glue that holds the family fabric together is worn out? Perhaps we can draw some inspiration from an African tale, which I sometimes tell.

The Lion and The Mouse
African-Adapted Aesop's tale

Before the desert was the desert there roamed the lion, elephant and crocodile. One day Simba the Lion was resting under a cool stand of sprawling trees when Lousy Mousy scampered over his back and waked him.

The grouchy Simba got up clasped Lousy Mousy under his paw and snarled.

—I'm going to eat you!

Poor Lousy Mousy implored his mercy, begging forgiveness. She pleaded.

—Please your Highness, do not stain your noble reputation with the blood of such a small and unworthy creature.

Simba was stirred by compassion and instantly freed his trembling captive.

Not long under African skies Simba the Great Hunter stumbled upon a hunters snare. He twisted and turned, this way and that way, and not being able to free himself, let out a thunderous roar. It pierced the jungle's canopy of darkness.

Lousy Mousy was still awake, recognized Simba's voice, scurried to his side and told him.

—Fear not for I am your friend.

Quickly, she with her sharp teeth gnawed through the knots and bonds and set Simba at liberty.

Our work of pulling together our tattered families has parallels to the African illustrations of the wee mouse's noble efforts in helping out the king of the jungle. How many times has a sense of inadequacy held us back off from doing what we really intended to do?

Next time, recall the moral of this story: irregardless to how small and insignificant we feel in a particular situation, we got something vital to offer. Just hang in there and keep gnawing. Be encouraged. Our family's breakthrough is coming. Can I get a witness! What a self-confidence booster, the story of the Lion and the Mouse has turned out to be for me on the journey.

Mature Adults

Restoring the family calls us to deeper waters. The story of one family, who witnessed the passing of a figure, bears this out. She was the last survivor from the bastion of aunts and uncles everyone knew and loved. She was a linchpin that held everybody together. She was a robust, healthy woman, though she maintained a quiet presence. She looked out for everyone. To help her called for a role reversal, as she progressed from walker to wheel chair. The younger folks stepped into those caring shoes.

Restoring the family calls us to maturity. Caregivers need to focus special attention on the conversion from immaturity to maturity. Dr. Henry Cloud, author of *Changes That Heal: How To Understand Your Past To Ensure a Healthier Future* (Zondervan Publishing, 1990) provides a list of qualities of mature adults.

▼ Reevaluate beliefs
▼ Disagree with authority figures
▼ See parents and authority figures realistically
▼ Make your own decisions
▼ Practice disagreeing
▼ Dealing with your own sexuality
▼ Give yourself permission to be equal with your parents
▼ Recognize and pursue talents
▼ Practice what you desire to excel

- ▼ Recognize the privileges of adulthood
- ▼ Discipline yourself
- ▼ Gain authority over evil
- ▼ Submit to others out of freedom
- ▼ Do good works
- ▼ Become a "Pharisee Buster"
- ▼ Appreciate mystery and the unknown

I personally have benefited from Dr. Cloud's lessons on my path to conversion from immaturity to maturity.

Operation Enduring Freedom

Mature adults extend themselves out of freedom to care. It was a joyous moment when our six-member immediate family received the Christian Family Award, which read "*and in you shall all the families in the earth shall be blessed*" (Genesis 12:3). Two years later, our family suddenly expanded to eight, as a result of Operation Enduring Freedom. (We became the guardians of our nephews, 11-year-old Shimannee and 16-year-old Demetrius, during their mom's military tour of duty in Iraq.) Yes, there was a sense of inadequacy on our part. But it was something that we felt the need to do.

Our lives dramatically changed, as you might well imagine. We now had six school-age children from grades one to twelve, every other grade represented. We as care providers slowed down, sought God's face, and made the necessary adjustments to not only accommodate yet nurture two more children. Of utmost importance, we received the high-energy boys as God's gifts. Yes, some things went wrong and even got broken around the house, as might be expected. More importantly, our love shone brighter.

What some possibly would have viewed, as a test of love's endurance actually helped us to be just a bit more caring. Meanwhile we have learned to be more patient and kind to one another. We daily were reminded of God's sacrificial love for us that would grant us the grace to extend ourselves and be that blessing to our nephews or all the families in the earth. Our experience brought us closer together and affirmed what caring means.

C=Commit to self-improvement

The eagle stirs up her nest with sharp, painful stones so that the eaglettes will soar.

If we commit to self-improvement, it will call us to shift the focus from others, acknowledging our own inner brokenness, drawing us to even deeper waters. Beginning your reflections, meditations, and thoughts in "Our Great Ideas Notebook" has been a first step in increasing self-awareness about understanding the past. Journal writing furthermore adds another good way to raise our level of self awareness. Here are a few practical tips for journal writing, which might be helpful.

1. Find a comfortable place where it is peaceful to reflect.

2. Date each entry. This comes in handy for reviewing your progress.

3. Avoid disruptions that break into your train of thought. For example, looking up word spellings, and correcting things.

4. Read over and reflect upon the journal entries whenever the feeling arises.

5. Be loose in when, how often and the format in which you write.

6. Be creative. Draw, scribble, pen a rap or poem. Just be you.

7. Let your expressions flow from the inner soul.

To commit to self-improvement is to practice conversion, as outlined under Key One in Chapter 11.

Begin to envision who you would like to be and your family to be, remembering that your healing and your families all are interconnected. Jot down your powerful vision. Make a drawing of it. Post the vision in a visible place that you will see every day. Speak it out loud daily.

"We are never healed alone." As earlier mentioned, Aeeshah Ababio-Clottey and Kokomon Clottey, authors of *Beyond Fear: Twelve Spiritual Keys to Racial Healing*, share, "We want to emphasize that whenever you heal yourself, you are healing your family, your local community, and ultimately the world we share."

Our healing—your healing and mine—has common threads. Both African and Native American cultures hold that our personal healing experience brings wholeness to the entire community.

A=Awake to the changing world

The mother giraffe kicks her newborn so that it will be able to stand in a dynamic world. She will muster up the strength to teach her calf to survive...otherwise it will perish.

If we awake to the changing world, it will invoke the courage to taste the daily salt of life. African-American females are one of the fastest growing groups getting infected with HIV. Hey, that's someone's sister, aunt, mother, or cousin! Let's rap about the issue. My work as an AIDS Educator has taken me to many shelters where women needed to be empowered.

Sample Job Description for Single Parent

Wanted: Energetic Individuals
(A typical single-parent job description)

Practitioner of family consumer science. Proficient in multi-level processing, time management, financial planning, home maintenance, cooking, and life skills. Requires patience, flexibility, perseverance, willingness to work overtime and ability to make new friends. Preference will be given to those who are

> *emotionally mature, having prior experience in coping with issues related to working overtime, guilt, loneliness, anxiety, and frustration. Loves children and adventure. Training in public safety, programming, conflict resolution, stress management and prevention a bonus. Other duties as assigned.*

Parenthood is an awesome responsibility for anyone, much more for singles.

As the single-parent job description attests, the job only begins in the labor room. Let's talk about the responsibility. Let's support one another as Big Brothers and Big Sisters.

Truth-telling about incarceration might sting a bit, but it will result in vital, intestinal fortitude. So many African-American males are incarcerated. Don't just sit by and act like there isn't anything happening. You can do something. We can ill afford to have our heads in the sand.

We simply have got to become more informed advocates for our families. John V. Elmore, a practicing criminal defense attorney provides a manual, a must read *Fighting for Your Life: The African-American Criminal Justice Survival Guide* (Amber Books 2004). So many brothers are disappointed in the system. It has historical roots.

Sharing brokenness will spark renewal. I was moved to gather a collection of testimonies about life issues. In my book *Healing is the Children's Bread: Complete with the Holistic Health Guide* are stories about the cool mask brothers wear, teens shooting one another, troubled relationships between parents and children.

Some stories are about teen parenting, the dragon of self-worthlessness, and mending broken promises. Other stories are about mental health, doing the right thing at the right time, and lessons in forgiving. The Problem/Opportunity Index points readers to vital resources. The stories can be used as a springboard to have non-threatening conversations about the real world.

We need to rap about real life situations. Basically, mistakes happen. But that doesn't spell it's the end of the world. We need to understand how alcoholic dependency in one generation may mask itself as chemical dependency in a later generation. It can be good to share hurts, disappointments, and misunderstandings in a non-threatening, nonjudgmental manner at an age-appropriate level. We need to hold out hope for our brothers and sisters.

R=Respect one another

If we respect one another, it will usher in a metamorphosis. From solitude the caterpillar springs forth a dazzling butterfly.

Sister Sledge popularized a song in the 1970s "We are Family." Let us embrace one family with a bouquet of differing views. Some family members are hands on. Others learn through experience. There are different personality types in all families. We all are broken vessels and have erred in our time. Yet, all are valuable to the mix.

Let us respect one another in our community. Let's be our brother's keeper and sister's keeper. I've rapped with brothers about abusing sisters. The bottom line was if you reach the end of your rope, you need to find other ways to work out your frustration. Similarly, we've taken time to make sure that we are taking care of our health.

Practicing conversion helps us focus on changing our behavior. In the family caregivers need to practice active listening with children. Parents, grandparents and other loved ones find more time to be tolerant. Encourage youth to express themselves, always remembering to be respectful of one another's views.

Open discussion about our passion, beliefs, values and motivation will go a long way in building a solid family. Pay close attention to what our youth say and do. Some of life's best lessons I've learned from children. They can provide us lessons in trust, child-like faith, and remind us what it means to be forgiving. Trusting God, our children and yours can join in celebrating abundant life.

E=Encourage life

Where rainbows end, there...re-creation begins.

Sample Family Mission Statement

To encourage the full spiritual, intellectual, physical, and emotional development of family members by fostering an atmosphere of love cooperation, unity and order; to build a home that encourages each family member to find and fulfill his or her God-given life purpose

A few years back our friend's family lacked direction and chose to get organized. They drafted a Family Mission and posted it in a visible place in their home. They put their heads together and soon blossomed. And if you need help, seek out counseling.

If we encourage life, it will lead us to pursue of our passions. The family is a living organism. Trusting God, our children and yours can join in celebrating abundant life. While healing begins in the inner depth of the soul in its final form there will be a clear, outward expression.

Three-Day Restoring the Family Gathering

Life crises are extraordinary moments that can spring the door open for change, as we witnessed. The passing of the last member from our parent's generation was a turning point, fur sure. It turned out to be a collective moment to reflect upon the past, which brought us closer together. The bottom line is the demystifying of adult, authority figure roles in our lives to see the person, good and imperfect, was an important first step to occur. We purposed to sow a gift from the heart of healthy relationships into our children's lives.

Time was set aside to elaborate upon the significance of honoring our elders in the African tradition, as the eldest family member was seated at the honor seat and presided over the ceremony. The elder presented recollections of the family. A highlight of the three-day "Restoring the Family Gathering" was our Love Tree Ceremony, held at the Black-owned concern, Zion's Daily Bread Family Restaurant. Besides relationship workshops, here are a few sample ideas for "Restoring the Family."

Rufus Tiefing Stevenson (kneeled center) joins Penn/Ohio group for "Restoring the Family" reeunion, Sharon, Pennsylvania.

Executive Meeting of the Mid-Atlantic Regional African-American Genealogy Groups, Philadelphia, Pennsylvania.

(Sample Restoring the Family Announcement)
Walker Family Reunion
(Restoring The Family)
July 9 – 11

...And in thee shall all families of the earth be blessed
Genesis 12:3

June 25,

Dear family members,

The Walker Family Reunion is fast approaching. The theme is "Restoring the Family." The idea of the reunion was inspired by conversation between Cousin Shuk, Cousin Cuff and Cousin Mico following the Homegoing Service of Aunt Ola. Please pass this announcement on to other family members.

Our directory with names, addresses and birthdates is still in progress. So please bring your address book.

The calendar of events, courtesy of Cousin Kofi, Program Chairperson, is enclosed. We have planned a lot of fun activities for all ages and are expecting a wonderful turnout.

We are a blessed family.

Love,

Uncle Slim and Aunt Emma Walker, Host and Hostess

(Sample Restoring the Family Announcement)

Jones Family Reunion
(Restoring The Family)
July 9 – 11

...And In Thee Shall All Families of the Earth Be Blessed
Genesis 12:3

Cousin Hester of Jackson, Mississippi will be giving the Special Reflections. Cousin Hester's talk, "Growing up with The Jones," will be presented at the Saturday Awards Dinner. Cousin Hester is the eldest family member.

Finally, we need to know who would be able to put up a few out of town family members. Give Paul and Shirley Jones, Reunion Host and Hostess, a call at (telephone number) or write and let us know as soon as possible. Thank you.

We love you.

What Makes A Christian Family?
Family Blessing

"May God Himself, the God of peace, sanctify you through and through. May your whole spirit, soul and body be kept blameless at the coming of our Lord Jesus Christ. The One who calls you is faithful and He will do it."
— I Thessalonians 5:23-24 (NIV)

Recipe For A Christian Family

Ingredients

1 sprig of Forget-Jesus-Not	1 dose of a Difference in opinion
2 broken vessels, Wholeheartedly surrendered	1 stalk Seasoned conversation
	Salty tears
1 Christian circle of loving family, neighbors and friends	1 tbs. Flowerettes of yesterdays passed
	3 tsp. Prayer, patience and time
1 bottle Cleansing Thoughts	Holy Spirit quick-acting-rising powder
2 ½ cups Love, peace and joy	Splash of Celebration
1 cup Wisdom and instruction	1 tsp. Extract of Goodness and Truth
¾ stick Daily reminders	Humor generously sprinkled
2 Equally-yoked believers	Fruit of the season
1 dash Firmness, faith, hope and love	
1 tsp. May I please, thank you, forgive me	

Tools: Gospel mixer, Marriage vow mold, Chastity cup, Power-of-agreement thermometer, Prayer wheel, Crockpot, Spatula of kindness, Family mission to serve.

Preparation: Measure 1 sprig of Forget-Jesus-Not, 2 broken vessels, Wholeheartedly surrendered, and 2 ½ cups Love, peace and joy. Add 1 Christian circle of loving family, neighbors and friends with Holy Spirit quick-acting-rising powder. Sift three times into a Chastity cup. Pour 1/3 bottle of Cleansing Thoughts. Chill, while keeping the prayer wheel turning.

Blend 2 Equally-yoked believers in the Gospel mixer. Add 1 dose of a Difference in opinion, 1 tsp. May I please, thank you, forgive me and Salty tears. Pour into Crockpot and let simmer five hours. Stir with Spatula of kindness every hour on the hour. Measure temperature (should not exceed boiling) with the Power-of-agreement thermometer on the fifth hour. Add 1 stalk Seasoned conversation, 3 tsp. Prayer, patience and time, and 1 tbs. Flowerettes of yesterdays passed. Let cool.

Inspect Chastity cup for purity before mixing 2 parts from Chastity cup to 1 part ingredients from crock pot in Gospel mixer bowl. Stir vigorously. Pour in 1 tsp. Extract of Goodness and Truth. Pour in a Marriage vow mold and add a splash of Celebration. Let cool until ready to serve.

For a delightful variation add Fruit after marriage. Flavor enhancers include 1 cup Wisdom and instruction, ¾ stick Daily reminders, a dash of Firmness, faith, hope and love, 2/3 bottle of Cleansing Thoughts and Humor generously sprinkled. Blend with the Family mission to serve.

Yield: A good marriage and a home for God's children of promise to grow and mature.

(Sample Restoring the Family Program)
Friday

Get Acquainted & Fun Night
Scripture Joel 2:25 – 27
Opening Prayer – Matthew Steverson
Song – TBA
Welcome – Drusilla Barksdale-Hall
Response by Naomi Steverson
Occasion – Roland Barksdale-Hall
Blessing of the food
Barbecue
Receive Family Information Pack
(Slide Show)
939 Baldwin Avenue, Suite 1
Sharon, PA

Olympic Fun Center
Family Fun
4070 E. State Street
Hermitage, PA

(Sample Restoring the Family Program)
Saturday

Love Power
Scripture Joel 2: 25-27
10:00 a.m. Opening Prayer – TBA
Song – Jesse T.C. Brown
10:00 a.m. Storytelling & Exhibit
10:30 a.m. – Noon Recreation & Love Power
Noon – 1:30 p.m. Taste of Steverson Contest
1:30 – 3:00 p.m. Heritage Tour
3:00 – 4:00 .m. Business Meeting
4:00 – 4:30 p.m. Parade & Tee-Shirt Contest
4:30 – 5:00 p.m. Photos

6:30 – 9:00 p.m.
Awards Banquet & Love Tree Ceremony
Zion's Daily Bread
841 Sharon-New Castle Road
Farrell, PA

(Sample Restoring the Family Program)
Sunday

Family Fellowship
Church Service
11:00 a.m. at Morris Chapel
926 Darr Avenue
Farrell, PA

After Service
Brunch will be served at
939 Baldwin Avenue
Sharon, PA

(Sample Love Power Activities)

▼ For the Saturday Craft, Parade and Tee-Shirt Contest children twelve and under should bring a white tee-shirt and fabric markers (optional).

▼ We are asking youth thirteen to eighteen to either design a family crest or write a family rap, song or poem for presentation at the Awards Dinner. (Dress is informal). Winning youth entry will appear on future family reunion tee-shirts. Craft, Parade and Tee-shirt Chairperson is Cousin Samantha (telephone number).

▼ We are requesting that you send copies of vintage (not originals) photographs along with a caption for the exhibit and "Name That Jones Game" by date. Please include a photo of yourself as a child. You can get copies made at Wal-Mart for a small charge.

▼ Also send copies of funeral home, wedding and baptismal programs for the family exhibit and archives. We are remembering our past. Please send to Linda Jones, Family Historian.

▼ On Saturday we are asking that everyone bring a covered special dish, dessert, salad or beverage (non-alcoholic please) for The Taste of Jones Contest. Bring a traditional family favorite with a recipe named in honor of a family member to swap and enter in the contest. Please write or call by date to let Cousin Sandra (telephone number) address to know what your entry will be.

▼ Let us know the names of recent high school, college and program graduates and the names of those who are retiring or celebrating an anniversary or birthday during the reunion weekend. We are honoring one another.

(Sample Love Power Packets)

A Taste of Healing Bread

A "kiss" …to remind us to love God and to be kind to other people.

A declaration …to encourage us to unfold your heritage, and learn lessons from our past.

A toothpick …to remind you to pick the lessons from our past to embrace and extend.

Salt …to acknowledge that the path to wholeness sometimes includes tears.

A crayon …to remind us to keep learning and creating.

A candle …to encourage us to rekindle our dreams.

A balloon …to remind us to celebrate life!

Love Power Packets are to be creative and hand-made, if possible, and reflect family member's unique character. Clip the Taste of Healing Bread, place in a baggie with a Hershey kiss, the Black Family Rap, a toothpick, packet of salt, colorful crayon, red candle, and bright balloon. Distribute your Taste of Healing Bread packets during Love Power festivities. Try serving up a savory dish of apple pie, peach cobbler, or pound cake alongside your Taste of Healing Bread packets. The Love Power festivities can culminate with a presentation of love packages to the elder, followed by other family members.

(Sample Love Power Note)

Dear Jesse,

You are an extraordinary man, and a precious husband to me. Life with you is sweet, satisfying and full of joy.

I thank God for uniting us together as one. And I look forward to many more precious times together.

Love Always,

Attention! Attention! Attention! For the Love Tree we are asking that you begin writing notes of love and appreciation to other family members in advance. This is a time to show how much you love your spouse, children, siblings, parents, aunts, uncles, grandparents and cousins. Take the opportunity to encourage someone in their special gift. Love packages will be sent to those who are unable to attend.

(Sample Family-Building Activities)

▼ Travel together. Take your children with you wherever you go. We recently visited the Pennsylvania State Capitol, where beautiful murals outline our early political leaders' religious views and understanding of tolerance. Knowing we belong with one another builds a home.

▼ Insist upon respecting elders in our community. Children should be required to send thank you pictures or letters when they receive any gift. Dr. Debra A. Henry's *Best Behavior: A Celebration of Good Manners for Our African-American Children* (Black Society Pages 2004) will reinforce the message. Love and respect builds a family.

▼ Instill positive values at home. At Sunday dinner you can select a scripture and call upon one of your children to expound upon it. Or select a story from Steven Barboza's *The African American Book of Values* (Doubleday 1998).

▼ Teach collective work and responsibility. On Saturday morning, everyone should have chores to do. Working together builds a family.

▼ Don't be afraid to repeat yourself. We were surprised by the benefit of repetition when one day, three-year-old Imanuel-Tiefing stood up and said to his bigger sister what he had heard so many times before, "No, Vonita, you have to say, 'Please, Imanuel, can I have some gum?'"

▼ Read books with family values and positive African-American images. A good start for children are books published by Just Us Books, owned by Wade and Cheryl Hudson, who have done a phenomenal job in getting the right types of materials out to our African-American children. Wade Hudson's classic *I Love My Family* is highly recommended. Your children will read if they see you reading.

▼ Post images from our history about visionary men and women. Emancipation 2000 (Madela Publishing www.emancipation2000.com) has a handsome poster depicting 120 African-American sheroes and heroes accompanied by a book with brief bios that will get your children to dream. Your children should be encouraged to be dream makers.

▼ Promote taking a stand against injustice and point out stellar community leaders. Children learn from their elders how to stand for the right thing.

▼ Expose your children to a variety of cultural activities. Your local arts guild provides drumming, jewelry making and other enrichment. Encourage music appreciation.

▼ Applaud each new endeavor. Our children, as well as their parents, enjoy a good celebration!

Life Applications To Ponder

1. How do you cope with the unknown and life transitions in family relations?

2. Reflect upon a time when you were in an awkward situation with an authority figure? How did you feel at the time? What was your response? Did you regain your composure and feel more at ease? What might you have done differently?

3. In what ways can you move beyond your present situation toward a more mature way of living?

4. There is comfort in pools of healing waters. Sharing stories of brokenness with others—who have been there—can help to cleanse your open wounds. Think about people who you would feel comfortable in confiding?

How are you using the healing and understanding that you have received to restore your family?

(Sample Evaluation Form)
The Jackson Restoring the Family Gathering
Evaluation Form

We need to hear from you in order to plan the next Restoring the Family Gathering. Please respond to the questions on the evaluation form and return to Richard Jackson, 815 High Street, Amherst, MA 16146 by August 1.

1. How many family reunions have you attended?

    ❑   0-1   ❑   2-4

    ❑   5-6   ❑   7 or more

2. In general, how satisfied or dissatisfied are you with the Restoring the Family Gathering?

    ❑   Completely Satisfied

    ❑   Mostly Satisfied

    ❑   Neither Satisfied Nor Dissatisfied

    ❑   Mostly Dissatisfied

    ❑   Completely Dissatisfied

3. What is your preference for the scheduling of future Restoring the Family Gatherings?

    ❑   Friday Evening and Saturday

    ❑   Saturday Only

    ❑   Friday Evening, Saturday and Sunday Morning

    ❑   Sunday Only

4. In generally, how often would you attend a Restoring the Family Gathering?

    ❑   once a year

    ❑   every four to five years

    ❑   every two to three years

    ❑   every six or more years

Comments:_____

Conclusion

Our families are a beautiful garden that we have been entrusted by the Creator to tend. With understanding of our past, let us steer a steady course on the path to restoration. Here's to your family, wishes of "Health, Wealth, and Success."

Peace be unto you,
Roland Barksdale-Hall

*Mr. Barksdale-Hall and his son, Drew, at the 2003
National Afro-American Historical and Genealogical Society
25th Anniversary Conference Banquet. Barskdale-Hall was*

Appendix A
African American Historical and Genealogical Societies

African American Historical and Genealogical Societies

The Afro-American Historical and Genealogical Society (AAHGS), has chapters and affiliates throughout the United States. As earlier mentioned, the author has a longstanding relationship with AAHGS. A life member of AAHGS, he is a founder of the AAHGS Pittsburgh and former book review editor for the scholarly *Journal of the Afro-American Historical and Genealogical Society.* AAHGS also publishes a bi-monthly newsletter. *Index to the Afro-American Historical and Genealogical Society Quarterly Issues of 1980-1990* is a valuable resource (see Beginning Black Genealogy Bibliography). The AAHGS annual conference, held during October, encourages scholarly research in Black history and genealogy.

The listing of African American Historical and Genealogical Societies first appeared in *Flower of the Forest: Black Genealogical Journal* 1 no. 6 (1987). A state-by-state updated listing of African American historical and genealogical societies follows. For the latest information on chapters, visit the AAHGS website www.aahgs.org

National Afro-American Historical and Genealogical Society, Inc. (AAHGS)
P.O. Box 73067
Washington, D.C. 20056-3067
www.aahgs.org

Alabama

AAHGS North Alabama
PO Box 89
Huntsville, Alabama 35762-0089

Arizona

AAHGS Tuscon
2501 North Goyette
Tucson, Arizona 85712-1934
<aztuscon.com/nonprofit/aahgs-tuscon/>

Black Family History Society
PO Box 1515
Gilbert, Arizona 85712

Arkansas

AAHGS Arkansas
PO Box 4294
Little Rock, Arkansas 72214
www.rootsweb.com~araags/

California

AAHGS Young Talented Achievers
PO Box 593
Rancho Cucamonga, California 91729
YTA4literacy@aol.com
www.inlandempireservices.com/ytahome.htm

African American Genealogical Society of Northern California (AAGSNC)
PO Box 27485
Oakland, California 94602-0985
www.aagscn.org

Publishes a quarterly newsletter, *From the Baobab Tree.* Holds meetings the third Saturday of each month, except July and August at the Dimond Branch of the Oakland Public Library.

Afro-American Genealogical Society
California Afro-American Museum
600 State Drive Exposition Park
Los Angeles, California 90037
Telephone: (213) 744-4050

Holds monthly meetings, usually the third Saturday at the California Afro-American Museum

California African American Genealogical Society
P.O. Box 8442
Los Angeles, California 90008-0442
lam.mus.ca.us/Africa/America/caags

Publishes *Heritage Newsletter.* Meets on the third or third Saturday of every month (except June and August) at the Martin Luther King Jr. United Methodist Church, 6625 4ᵗʰ Avenue, Los Angeles, California 90047. Sponsors workshops and an annual Juneteenth Celebration.

Colorado

Black Genealogy Search Group of Denver
P.O. Box 40674
Denver, Colorado 80204-0674

Publishes *Black Tracks.* The Search Group (also known as the Black Genealogy Research Group) collects and disseminates black genealogical information through monthly meetings (except August and December) at the Ford-Warren Branch of the Denver Public Library. Projects include a resource file, surname/locality cross reference file, and a beginner's kit for genealogist.

District of Columbia

AAHGS James Dent Walker
PO Box 60632
Washington, DC 20039-0632

Florida

AAHGS Central Florida
PO Box 1347
Orlando, Florida 32802-1347
www.rootsweb.com-flcfaahg

AAHGS Tampa
PO Box 1182
Valrico, Florida 33595-1182

Georgia

AAHGS Metro
PO Box 54063
Atlanta, Georgia 30308
www.rootsweb.com/~gaahgs/

African American Family History Association (AAFHA)
P.O. Box 115268
Atlanta, Georgia 30310

AAFHA publishes a quarterly newsletter, *Homecoming: African American Family History in Georgia* (1982), and *Slave Bills of Sale Project* (1986). Gives Annual Alex Haley Literary Award. Holds quarterly meetings in January, April, July, and October.

Illinois

AAHGS Little Egypt
PO Box 974
Carbondale, Illinois 62901

AAHGS Patricia Liddell Researchers
PO Box 438652
Chicago, Illinois 60643
plraahgs@hotmail.com
<family.freesitenow.com/plr>

AAHGS Northern Illinois Regional
PO Box 478
Cherry Valley, Illinois 61016-0478
AAHGS-NIRC@hotmail.com

Afro-American Genealogical and Historical Society of Chicago (AAGHSC)
740 E 56th Place
Chicago, Illinois 60637

Publishes an *AAGHSC Newsletter.* Meets the second Sunday of every month and sponsors an annual February conference.

Maryland

AAHGS Baltimore
PO Box 9366
Baltimore, Maryland 21228

AAHGS Central Maryland
PO Box 648
Columbia, Maryland 21045

AAHGS Prince George's County
PO Box 44252
Ft. Washington, Maryland 20744-4252

Massachusetts

AAHGS New England
PO Box 166
Burlington, Massachusetts 01803

Michigan

Fred Hart Williams Genealogical Society
Detroit Public Library
Burton Historical Collection
5201 Woodward Avenue
Detroit, Michigan 48202
www.fhwgs.org

Publishes a quarterly newsletter and *Our Untold Stories: A Collection of Family History Narratives* (1993). Meets monthly from September to June (excluding December) in the Explorer Room, Detroit Public Library.

Missouri

AAHGS Landon Cheek
PO Box 210625
St. Louis. Missouri 63121

New Jersey

AAHGS New Jersey
PO Box 237
Jersey City, New Jersey 07303
njcaahgs@aol.com

New York

AAHGS Jean Sampson Scott Greater New York
PO Box 022340
Brooklyn, New York 11201-0049
www.aahgsny.org

North Carolina

AAHGS North Carolina/Piedmont Triad
PO Box 36254
Greensboro, North Carolina 27416
www.people-places.com/aahgs

Ohio

African-American Genealogical Society of Cleveland (AAGSC)
P.O. Box 200382
Cleveland, Ohio 44120

Publishes a quarterly newsletter. Projects include an indexing of obituaries in *The Call and Post*. Meets on the fourth Saturday of each month (except August and December) at Maple Heights Public Library.

Oberlin African-American Genealogy and History Group
MPO 0374
Oberlin, Ohio 44074-0374
www.geocities.com/oberlinaagenealogy/

Pennsylvania

AAHGS Family Quest Society
(Philadelphia)
PO Box 2272
Bala Cynwyd, Pennsylvania 19004
aahgsfamilyquest@aol.com

AAHGS Pittsburgh
PO Box 5707
Pittsburgh, Pennsylvania 15208
aahgspgh08@aol.com

African-American Genealogy Group
P.O. Box 1798
Philadelphia, Pennsylvania 19105

Publishes a quarterly newsletter. Meets on the fourth Tuesday of each month.

Tennessee

African American Genealogical and Historical Society (AAGHS)
PO Box 1711124
Nashville, TN 37217

Texas

AAHGS Texas
T.S.U. Box #1109
3100 Cleburne
Houston, Texas 77004
aahgs-htown@sbcglobal.net

African American Genealogical and Historical Society (AAGHS) of San
Antonio, Inc.
PO Box 200784
San Antonio, TX 78220
www.rootsweb.com/~txbexar/aaghs.htm

Holds meetings on the 1st Saturday of the month at the San Antonio
Central Library

Tarrant County Black History and Genealogical Society
1020 East Humboldt
Fort Worth, Texas 76104

Publishes a newsletter and/or a quarterly publication.

Virginia

AAHGS African American Genealogical Group of
Charlottesville/Albemarle County
40 Chippewa Lane
Palmyra, Virginia 22973

AAHGS Hampton Roads
PO Box 2448
Newport News, Virginia 23609-2448

Wisconsin

Afro-American Genealogical Society of Milwaukee
5195 N. 64th Street
Milwaukee, Wisconsin 53218
www.rootsweb.com~wiaagsm

Holds meetings at the Martin Luther King Library on the third Saturday of the month. (Meeting site changes during the summer.)

African American Lineage Societies

American Society of Freedmen's Descendants (ASFD)
c/o USCTI for Local History and Family Research
Office of Academic Affairs
Hartwick College
Oneonta, New York 13820
Matthewsh@hartwick.edu

The United States Colored Troops Institute (USCTI) for Local History and Family Research, sponsor of the USCT Institute, maintains a USCT database, publishes the *USCT Civil War Digest*, and has numerous affiliates, including the lineage society American Society of Freedmen's Descendants (ASFD). Certified membership to the ASFD is open to anyone who can prove freedmen ancestry in the 1870 U.S. census.

The International Society of Sons and Daughters of Slave Ancestry (ISDSA)
PO Box 436937
Chicago, Illinois 60643-6937
ISDSA@aol.com
www.rootsweb.com/~ilissdsa

ISDSA maintains a database, publishes a newsletter, and promotes education through a traveling exhibit, "A Tribute to Our Enslaved Ancestors." Certified membership, based upon documented lineage to a slave ancestor, is open to any individuals without regard to sex, race, color, creed, or national origin.

A, B, C's of Genealogy

This bibliography was compiled for a library science course on Black Bibliography with Professor Wendell Wray at the University of Pittsburgh in 1983. It has gone through subsequent versions, being updated for a seminar on African American genealogy that the author presented at the George Peabody Library of Johns Hopkins University on Saturday, October 24, 1987. The version appearing here was drawn from the author's collection, Hillman Library of the University of Pittsburgh, Milton S. Eisenhower Library of Johns Hopkins University, Shenango Valley Community Public Library, Allen County Public Library, and the Newberry Library. Check your local library for out of print materials. Consult your librarian about interlibrary loan services.

Abajian, James de T. *Blacks in Selected* Newspapers, Censuses and other Sources: An Index to Names and Subjects. Boston: G.K. Hall, 1977. This is a three volume set.

Beasley, Donna. *Family Pride: The Complete Guide to Tracing African-American Genealogy.* New York: Macmillan Books, 1997. Reprinted by IDG Books Worldwide.

Beller, Susan Provost. *Roots for Kids: A Genealogy Guide for Young People.* White Hall: Betterway Publications, 1989. Book developed out a twelve week course that the author taught her fourth grade class.

Blockson, Charles L. with Ron Fry. *Black Genealogy.* Englewood Cliffs: Prentice-Hall, 1977. This classic, Black Classic Press has reprinted.

Brown, Vandella. *Celebrating the Family: Steps to Planning a Family Reunion.* Salt Lake City: Ancestry, 1991. Focuses upon planning with helpful checklists and sample letters.

Burroughs, Tony. *Black Roots.* New York: Fireside Books, 2001. Intermediate level.

Byers, Paula K., editor. *African American Genealogical Source Book* (7th edition). Detroit: Gale Research, 1995 (out of print). Advanced level, as viewed through subject contributors' presentations on various research topics.

Carmack, Sharon Debartolo. *Your Guide to Cemetery Research.* Cincinnati: Betterway Books, 2002.

Chuka-Oris, Oganna. *Names from Africa.* Chicago: Johnson Publishing, 1972.

Crawford-Oppenheimer, Christine. *Long-Distance Genealogy.* Cincinnati: Betterway Books, 2000. Outlines how to do genealogy from home.

Croom, Emily Anne. *The Genealogist's Companion and Sourcebook: Guide to the Resources You Need for Unpuzzling Your Past.* (2nd edition). Cincinnati: Betterway Books, 2003.

Croom, Emily Anne. *Unpuzzling Your Past: the Best-Selling Basic Guide to Genealogy.* (4th edition). Cincinnati: Betterway Books, 2001.

Crowe, Elizabeth Powell. *Genealogy Online.* New York: McGraw-Hill, 2003.

Crume, Rick. *Plugging into Your Past: How to Find Real Family History Records Online.* Cincinnati: Betterway Books, 2004.

Curtis, Nancy C. *Black Heritage Sites: An African American Odyssey and Finder's Guide.* American Library Association: Chicago, 1996.

Everton, George B., Sr., editor. *The Handy Book for Genealogists.* (6th edition) Utah, Everton Publishers, 1971. Lists name changes for counties, census and mortality schedules, archives, libraries, and societies.

Fletcher, William. *Recording Your Family History.* New York, Dodd, Mead and Company, 1986. (out of print) Offers various themes and interview questions.

Garro, Susan P. *Black Studies: A Select Catalog of National Archives Microfilm Publications.* Washington, DC: National Archives, 1984.

Ginsburg, Ralph. *100 Years of Lynching*. Baltimore: Black Classic Press, 1969, 1988.

Goodwin, Maria R. *Precious Memories: A Basic Guide for Collecting Family History*. Washington, DC: Smithsonian Institution Anacostia Museum and Center for African American History and Culture, 2002.

Haley, Alex. "Black History, Oral History, and Genealogy," *Oral History Review* (1973).

Hinckley, Kathleen W. *Locating Lost Family Members and Friends: Modern Genealogical Research Techniques for Locating the People of Your Past and Present*. Cincinnati: Betterway Books, 1999.

Hornsby, Alton. *Chronology of African-American History: Significant Events and People from 1619 to the Present*. Detroit: Gale Research, 1991.

Katz, William Loren, *Black Indians: A Hidden Heritage*. Atheneun: New York, 1986.

Lawson, Sandra. *Generations Past: A Selected List of Sources for Afro-American Genealogical Research*. Washington, DC: Library of Congress, 1988. (out of print) Highlights research sources available at the Library of Congress.

Linder, Bill R. "Black Genealogy: Basic Steps to Research," *History News* 36 (February 1981).

My History Is America's History: 15 Things You Can Do To Save America's Stories. Washington, DC: National Endowment for the Humanities, 1999.

Newman, Debra L. *Black History: A Guide to Civilian Records in the National Archives*. Washington, DC: National Archives Trust Fund Board, General Service Administration, 1984.

Newman, Debra L. *List of Free Black Heads of Families in the First Census of the United States 1790*. National Archives Special List No. 34, Washington, DC, 1974.

Newnan-Coweta Historical Society. *Coweta County, Georgia Marriages 1827-1979.* Roswell, Georgia: WH Wolfe Associates, 1981. (two volumes) Black marriages, which span from 1866 to 1979, are contained in volume 2.

Newnan-Coweta Historical Society. *A History of Coweta County, Georgia.* Roswell, Georgia: WH Wolfe Associates, 1988.

Picott, J. Rupert. "Tracing Your Roots," *Negro History Bulletin* 41 (January 1978).

Ploski, Harry A. *Negro Almanac: A Reference Work on the African-American.* (5th edition) Detroit: Gale Research, 1989.

Pope-Hennessy, James. *Sins of the Fathers: A Study of the Atlantic Slave Traders 1441-1807.* New York: Alfred A. Knopf, 1967. (out of print)

Redford, Dorothy Spruill. *Somerset Homecoming: Recovering A Lost Heritage.* New York: Doubleday, 1988.

Rose, Christine. *Family Associations: Organization and Management* (3rd edition). San Jose: Rose Family Association, 2001.

Rose, James M. and Alice Eichholz. *Black Genesis: A Resource Book for African-American Genealogy* (2nd edition). Baltimore, Genealogical Publishing, 2003. Updated state-by-state resource lists.

Scott, Emmett J. *Negro Migration During the War.* New York: Arno Press, 1920, 1969.

Scott, Jean Sampson. *Beginning an Afro-American Genealogical Pursuit.* New York: Eppress Printers, 1985.

Smith, Jessie Carney. *Ethnic Genealogy: A Research Guide.* Westport: Greenwood Press, 1983. Covers multi-ethnic resources.

Smolenyak, Megan and Ann Turner. *Trace Your Roots with DNA: Using Genetic Tests to Explore Your Family Tree.* Emmaus: Rodale, 2004.

Stewart, Julia. *African Names: Names from the African Continent for Children and Adults.* Citadel Press, 1996.

Sturdivant, Katherine Scott. *Organizing and Preserving Your Heirloom Documents.* Cincinnati: Betterway Books, 2002. Discusses transcription and indexing of documents.

United States National Archives and Records Administration. *Black Studies: Select Catalog of National Archives Microfilm Publications.* Washington, DC: National Archives Trust Fund Board, General Service Administration, 1984.

Uya, Okon Edet. "Using Federal Archives: Some problems in Doing Research," in *Afro-American History: Sources for Research.* Edited by Robert L. Clarke. Washington, DC: Howard University Press, 1981.

Walker, Barbara D. *Index to the Journal of the Afro-American Historical and Genealogical Society Quarterly: Issues of 1980 – 1990.* Bowie: Heritage Books, 1991.

Walker, James D. *Black Genealogy: How to Begin.* Athens, GA: University of Georgia Center for Continuing Education, 1977.

Walton-Raji, Angela Y. *Black Indian Genealogy Research.* Bowie: Heritage Books, 1993.

Westin, Jeanne Eddy. *Finding You Roots.* New York: Ballantine, 1989.

Where to Write for Vital Records. Hyattsville: U.S. Department of Health and Human Services, 1993. Available for sale from the U.S. Government Printing Office and government bookstores.

Who's Who Among African Americans.

Witcher, Curt Bryan. *African American Genealogy: A Bibliography and Guide to Sources.* Fort Wayne: Round Tower Books, 2000.

Woodson, Carter G. *Free Heads of Families in the United States Census of 1830.* Washington, DC: Association for the Study of Negro Life and History, 1925.

Woodtor, Dee Parmer. *Finding a Place Called Home: A Guide To African-American Genealogy and Historical Identity.* New York: Random House, 1999. Intermediate level.

Wright, Roberta Hughes and Wilbur Hughes III. *Lay Down Body: Living History in African-American Cemeteries.* Detroit: Visible Ink, 1996.

Young, Tommie Morton. *Afro-American Genealogy Sourcebook.* New York: Garland Publishing, 1987.

From Slavery To Freedom

Alford, Terry. *Prince Among Slaves.* New York: Harcourt Brace Jovanovich, Inc., 1977.

Bentley, George R. *A History of the Freedmen's Bureau.* Philadelphia: Octagon Books, 1970.

Berlin, Ira. *Slaves Without Masters.* New York: Pantheon Books, 1974.

Clayton, Robert. Cash For Blood: The Baltimore to New Orleans Domestic Slave Trade. Bowie: Heritage Books, 2002.

Franklin, John Hope and Alfred A. Moss, Jr. *From Slavery to Freedom* (8th edition). New York: Alfred A. Knopf, 2000.

Genovese, Eugene D. *Roll, Jordan, Roll: The World the Slaves Made.* New York, Pantheon Books, 1974.

Gross-Moore, Frances. "The Origins of the Gullah Language," *Journal of the Afro-American Historical and Genealogical Society,* vol. 21 no. 2, (2002).

Gutman, Herbert G. *The Black Family in Slavery and Freedom, 1750-1925.* New York: Vintage Books, 1976.

Jones, Jacqueline. *Labor of Love, Labor of Sorrow: Black Women, Work and the Family, From Slavery to the Present.* New York: Basic Books, 1985.

Katz, William Loren. *The Black West: A Documentary and Pictorial History.* Garden City: Doubleday, 1971.

Lincoln, Eric C. and Lawrence H. Mamiya. *The Black Church in the African American Perspective.* Durham: Duke University, 1990.

Mannix, Daniel P. *Black Cargoes: A History of the Atlantic Slave Trade.* New York: Viking Press, 1962.

Shaw, Robert B. *A Legal History of Slavery in the United States*. Bowie, Heritage Books, 1991.

Siebert, Wilbur H. *The Underground Railroad from Slavery to Freedom*. North Stratford: Ayer Company Publishers, 1898, 2000. Contains a valuable list of operators, African American operators being indicated.

Still, William. *The Underground Railroad*. Chicago: Johnson Publishing, 1871, 1970. Includes biographical information of fugitive slaves.

Thomas, Kenneth H. "A Note on the Pitfalls of Black Genealogy: The Origins of Black Surnames," *Georgia Archives* 6 (spring 1978).

Thomas, Velma Maia, *Lest We Forget: The Passage From Africa to Slavery and Emancipation*. New York: Crown Publishers, 1997.

Military

Barth, Chuck, *Due Reward: The Story of the Buffalo Soldiers from 1866 to 1896*. Tucson: Blue Horse Productions, 2000.

Blackett, R.J.M. *Thomas Morris Chester, Black Civil War Correspondent: His Dispatches from the Virginia Front*. Baton Rouge: Louisiana state University Press, 1989.

Gladstone, William A. *United States Colored Troops, 1863-1867*. Gettysburg: Thomas Publications, 1990.

Gourdin, J. Raymond. "Name Changing Since the Civil War: A Case of Three USCT Regiments from South Carolina," *Journal of the Afro-American Historical and Genealogical Society* vol. 21 no. 1 (2002).

Ham, Debra Newman. "Guide to Records about Black Participants in the American Revolution from the War Department Collection of Revolutionary War Records at the National Archives and Records Administration," *Journal of the Afro-American Historical and Genealogical Society* vol. 22 no. 1 (2003).

Lee, Irvin H. *Negro Medal of Honor Men*. New York: Dodd, Mead, and Co., 1967.

National Genealogical Society. *Index of Revolutionary War Pension Applications*. Washington, DC: National Archives, 1976.

Newman, Debra L. *List of Black Servicemen, Compiled from the War Department's Collection of Revolutionary War Records.* Special List No. 36, Washington, DC, 1974.

Schweitzer, George K. *Civil War Genealogy: A Basic Research Guide for Tracing Your Civil War Ancestors with Detailed Sources and Precise Instructions for Obtaining Information from Them.* Knoxville: GK Schweitzer, 1988.

Secret, Jeannette Braxton. *Guide to Tracing Your African American Civil War Ancestor.* Bowie: Heritage Books, 1997.

USCT Civil War Digest. Published semiannually by the United States Colored Troops Institute for Local History and Family Research, Associate Dean/USCT Institute, Center for Interdependence, Hartwick College, Oneonta, New York 13820. (vol. 1, no. 1 1999 —). Subscription is available with annual dues.

Memoirs

Adams, Willam Crawford Samuel. *Free Born: 350 Years of Eastern Shore African American History.* Bowie: Heritage Books, 2000.

Berry, Leonidas H. *I Wouldn't Take Nothin' For My Journey: Two Centuries of an Afro-American Minister's Family.* Chicago: Johnson Publishing, 1981.

Buckley, Gail Shumate. *The Hornes: An American Family.* New York, Plume Book, 1986.

Comer, James P. *Maggie's American Dream: The Life and Times of a Black Family.* New York: New American Library Books, 1988.

Darden, Norma Jean and Carole Darden. *Spoonbread and Strawberry Wine.* New York: W.W. Norton, 1984.

Golden, Lily. *My Long Journey Home.* Chicago: Third World Press, 2003.

Haley, Alex. *Roots: Te Saga of an American Family.* Garden City: Doubleday, 1976.

Hicks, Nora Louise. *Slave Girl Reba and her Descendants in America.* [self-published] 1974.

Ione, Carole. *Pride of Family: Four Generations of American Women of Color.* New York: Summit Books, 1991.

Khanga, Yelena. *Soul to Soul: the Story of a Black Russian American Family 1865-1992.* New York: W.W. Norton, 1992.

Morgan, Kathryn L. *Children of Strangers: The Stories of a Black Family.* Philadelphia: Temple University Press, 1981.

Murray, Pauli. *Proud Shoes: the Story of an American Family.* New York: Harper and Row, 1956, 1978.

The Quanders United Tricentennial Celebration 1684-1984. Washington, DC: The Quanders United Incorporated, 1984.

Taulbert, Clifton L. *When We Were Colored.* New York: Penguin Books, 1995.

Disparities

Barksdale-Hall, Roland. *Healing is the Children's Bread: Complete with the Holistic Health Guide.* Sharon: Best, 1999.

Cloud, Henry. *Changes That Heal: How To Understand Your Past To Ensure A Healthier Future.* Grand Rapids: Zondervan Publishing, 1990.

Cobb, W. Montague. "Hospital Integration in the United States," *Journal of the National Medical Association,* 55 no. 4 (1963).

Edelman, Marian Wright. *The Measure of Success: A Letter to My Children and Yours.* New York: Harper Perennial, 1992.

Hollies, Linda H. *Inner Healing for Broken Vessels: Seven Steps to Mending Childhood Wounds.* New York: Welstar, 1990.

Krause, Carol. *How Healthy Is Your Family Tree? A Complete Guide to Tracing Your Family's Medical and Behavioral Tree.* New York: Fireside Book, 1995.

Kunjufu, Jawanza. *Developing Positive Self-Images and Discipline in Black Children.* Chicago: African American Images, 1984.

Majors, Richard, and Janet Mancini Billson. *Cool Pose: the Dilemmas of Black Manhood in America.* Atlanta: Longstreet, 1992.

Perkins, Spencer, and Chris Rice. *More Than Equals: Racial healing for the Sake of the Gospel.* Downers Grove: InterVarsity Press, 1993.

Ralston, Bruce L. "I Swear by Imhotep the Physician," *New York State Journal of Medicine* 77 no. 13 (1977).

Saunders, John B. de C. M. *The Transition from Ancient Egyptian to Greek Medicine.* Lawrence: University of Kansas Press, 1963.

Segy, Ladislas. "The African Attitude toward Sickness Its Relation to Sculpture," Acta. Trop, 31 no. 4 (1974).

"Seventh Imhotep National Conference on Hospital Integration," *Journal of the National Medical Association*, 55 no. 4 (1963).

"Sixth Imhotep Conference Confident of Results from United Broad Effort," *Journal of the National Medical Association*, 54 no. 4 (1962).

Weems, Renita J. *I Asked for Intimacy: Stories of Blessing, Betrayals, and Birthings.* San Diego: LuraMedia, 1993.

Williams, Richard Allen. *Textbook of Black-Related Disease.* New York: Mc-Graw-Hill, 1975.

State-By-State Resources

Alabama

Pinkard, Ophelia Taylor and Barbara Clayton Clark. *Descendants of Shandy Wesley Jones and Evalina Love Jones: the Story of an African American Family of Tuscaloosa, Alabama.* Baltimore: Gateway Press, 1993.

Arkansas

Kearney, Janis F. *Cotton Field of Dreams: A Memoir.* Chicago: Writing Our Own Word Press, 2004.

Pegues, Hazel D., compiler. "A Report of the Negro High Schools of Ft. Smith, Arkansas," *The Frontier Freedman's Journal* 1 no. 1 (1992).

Patterson, Ruth Polk. *The Seed of Sally Good'n: A Black Family of Arkansas 1833-1953.* Lexington: University Press of Kentucky, 1985.

Walton-Raji, Angela. "Indian Freedman Genealogy: Indian Freedman Testimonies Serving as Critical Guides to Black Family History," *The Frontier Freedman's Journal* 1 no. 1 (1992).

District of Columbia

Pinkett, Harold T. *National Church of Zion Methodism: A History of John Wesley A.M.E. Zion Church, Washington, DC.* Baltimore, Gateway Press, 1989.

Provine, Dorothy S. *District of Columbia Free Negro Registers, 1821-1861.* Bowie: Heritage Books, 1996. This is a two volume set.

Sluby, Paul E., editor. *History of Plymouth Congregational Church United Church of Christ.* Washington, DC: Plymouth Congregational Church, 1997.

Florida

Fears, Mary L. Jackson. *Slave Ancestral Research: It's Something Else.* Bowie, Heritage Books, 1995.

Mitchell, Olga Fenton and Gloria Fenton Magbie. *The Life and Times of Joseph E. Clark: From Slavery to Town Father (Eatonville, Florida).* Jonesboro, Arkansas: FOUR-G Publishers, 2003.

Georgia

Crook, Ray and et al. *Sapelo Voices: Historical Anthropology and the Oral Traditions of Gullah-Geechee Communities on Sapelo Island, Georgia.* Carrollton: State University of West Georgia, 2003.

Martin, Joann, editor. *Slave Bills of Sale Project.* Atlanta: African-American Family History Association, 1986. This is a two volume set.

Merritt, Carole. *Homecoming: African-American Family History in Georgia.* Atlanta: Atlanta: African-American Family History Association, 1982.

Stewart, Roma Jones. *Africans in Georgia 1870.* Chicago: Homeland Publications, 1993.

Schwartz, Tony. "The Negro Boy Alfred," *Newsweek*, July 4, 1977, p. 29.

Temple, Sarah Blackwell Gober. *The First Hundred Years: A Short History of Cobb County, in Georgia.* (5th edition) Atlanta: Cherokee Publishing Company, 1980. Chapter 14 "Slaves and Agriculture" listed names of slaves found in a few estate records.

Wagner, Clarence M. *Profiles of Black Georgia Baptists.* Atlanta: Bennett Brothers Printing, 1980.

Wynne, Frances Holloway. "Slave Importation Lists from Richmond County, Georgia, 1820-1821," *Journal of the Afro-American Historical and Genealogical Society* 18 no. 2 (1999).

Hawaii

Jackson, Miles M., editor. *They Followed the Trade Winds: African Americans in Hawaii.* Honolulu: University of Hawaii Press, 2005.

Illinois

Alabama Study Group of the Afro-American Genealogical and Historical Society of Chicago. *An Index of Headstones in Lincoln Cemetery, Chicago, Illinois.* Bowie: Heritage Books, 1999.

Thackeray, David. *Afro-American Family History at the Newberry Library: A Research Guide and Bibliography.* Chicago: Newberry Library, 1988.

Tregillis, Helen Cox. *River Roads to Freedom: Fugitive Slave Notices and Sheriff Notices Found in Illinois Sources.* Bowie: Heritage Books, 1988.

Indiana

Bigham, Darrel E. *We Ask Only a Fair Trial: A History of the Black Community of Evansville, Indiana.* Bloomington: Indiana University Press, 1987.

Spears, Jean E. and Dorothy Paul, transcribers. *Admission Record Indianapolis Asylum for Friendless Colored Children, 1871-1900.* Family History and Genealogy Section, Indiana Historical Society, Indianapolis, Indiana, 1978.

Witcher, Curt Bryan. *Bibliography of Sources for Black Family History in the Allen County Public Library Genealogy Branch.* Fort Wayne: Allen County Public Library, 1989.

Kentucky

Kentucky's Black Heritage: The Role of the Black People in the History of Kentucky from Pioneer Days to the Present. Frankfort, Commonwealth of Kentucky, Kentucky Commission on Human rights, 1971.

Neuforth, Karen P. "Generations: The Family and Ancestry of Oscar Micheaux," *Journal of the Afro-American Historical and Genealogical Society* 21 no. 1 (2002).

Schmitzer, Jeanne Cannella. "Name Index to the Registers of Depositors in the Lexington, Kentucky Branch of the Freedmen's Savings and Trust Company," *Journal of the Afro-American Historical and Genealogical Society* 14 nos. 1 & 2 (1995).

Streets, David H. *Slave Genealogy: A Research Guide with Case Studies.* Bowie, Heritage Books, 1986.

Walker, James Dent. "Kentucky Marriage Records," *Journal of the Afro-American Historical and Genealogical Society* 1 (summer 1980).

Louisiana

Hardy, Linell H. *Abstract of Account Information of Freedman's Savings and Trust, New Orleans, Louisiana, 1866-1869.* Bowie: Heritage Books, 1999.

Schafer, Judith Kelleher. *Slavery, the Civil Law, and the Supreme Court of Louisiana.* Baton Rouge: Louisiana State University Press, 1994.

Washington, Edwin B, Jr. "Using Microsoft Office ® to Access the Louisiana Slave Databases," *Journal of the Afro-American Historical and Genealogical Society* 21, no. 1 (2002).

Wainwright, Irene. "African-American Genealogical Sources in the Louisiana Division of the New Orleans Public Library," *Journal of the Afro-American Historical and Genealogical Society* 19, no. 2 (2000).

Maryland

Callum, Agnes Kane. *Colored Volunteers of Maryland Civil War 7th Regiment United States Colored Troops 1863-1866*. Baltimore: Mullac Publishers, 1990.

Clayton, Ralph. *Black Baltimore, 1820-1870*. Bowie, Heritage Books, 1987.

—, *Slavery, Slaveholding, and the Free Black Population of Antebellum Baltimore*. Bowie, Heritage Books, 1993.

Douglas, Joseph L. "Harriet Bailey: Presumed Sister of Frederick Douglas," *Journal of the Afro-American Historical and Genealogical Society* 21 no. 1 (2002).

Jacobsen, Phebe R. *Researching Black Families at the Maryland Hall of Records*. Annapolis: Maryland Hall of Records, 1984.

Lancaster, R. Kent and Jenny Masur. "Ridgely Slaves 1829," *Flower of the Forest Black Genealogical Journal* 2 no. 3 (1996).

Michigan

Warren, Frances H., compiler. *Michigan Manual of Freedmen's Progress*. Detroit: , 1915.

Mississippi

Craighead, Sandra G. "Index and Analysis of Mississippi Marriages Performed by Freedmen's Bureau Field Offices in 1865," *PLR News Journal* 3 no. 1 (1996).

New Jersey

Dickenson, Richard. "The Vanarsdale of Princeton, New Jersey," *The Jersey Heritage* l 2 no. 1 (1994).

Jersey Heritage. Published by the New Jersey Chapter, Afro-American Historical and Genealogical Society, P.O. Box 237, Jersey City, New Jersey 07303. (vol. 1, no. 1 1992 —).

Lutkins, Allen. "Dunkerhook: Slave Community?" *Journal of the Afro-American Historical and Genealogical Society* 21 no. 1 (2002).

Wright, Giles R. *Afro-Americans in New Jersey.* Trenton: New Jersey Historical Commission, Department of State, 1988.

New York

Dickenson, Richard B. "Staten Island Colonial Slaves In Wills and Manumissions of Richmond County, New York," *Journal of the Afro-American Historical and Genealogical Society* 23 no. 1 (2004).

Harris, Augustus W. "Documenting Samuel Anderson Quite Possibly the Last Slave of Flatbush Town," *Journal of the Afro-American Historical and Genealogical Society* 20 no. 1 (2000).

Matthews, Harry Bradshaw. *Honoring New York's Forgotten Soldiers: African Americans of the Civil War.* Oneonta: Hartwick College, 1998.

Swans, Robert J. "The Black Population of New Netherland: As Extracted from the Records of Baptisms and Marriages of the Dutch Reformed Church (New York City), 1630-1664," *Journal of the Afro-American Historical and Genealogical Society* 14 nos. 1 & 2 (1995).

North Carolina

Blackman, A.M. *Cohabitation Records of Davie County, North Carolina, 1866.* Clemmons: A.M. Blackman, 1987.

McBride, Ransom. "Searching for the Past of the North Carolina Black Family in Local, Regional, and Federal Record Resources," *North Carolina Genealogical Society Journal* 9 (May 1993).

Byrd, William L III. *North Carolina Slaves and Free Persons of Color: Chowan County, Vol. 2.* Bowie: Heritage Books, 2003. Seventh volume in this series.

Peebles, Minnie. "Black Genealogy," *North Carolina Historical Review* 55 (April 1978).

White, Barneta McGhee. *In Search of Kith and Kin: The History of a Southern Black Family.* Baltimore: Gateway Press, 1986.

Yellin, Jean Fagan. *Harriet Jacobs: A Life.* New York: Basic Civitas Books, 2004.

Young, Tommie M. "Ten Steps in Rooting Out the Past of the Black Family," 6 no. 2 August 1980).

Ohio
Davis, Russell H. *Black Americans in Cleveland: From George Peake to Carl B. Stokes.* Washington, DC: Associated Publishers, 1972, 1985.

Bardes, Eleanor Dooks and Mary H. Remler. *Hamilton County, Ohio, Burial Records, Vol. 9, Union Baptist African American Cemetery.* Bowie: Heritage Books, 1997. The Union Baptist Church, founded in 1831, is one of the oldest African American Baptist churches in Ohio.

Peskin, Allan, ed. *North into Freedom: the Autobiography of John Malvin, Free Negro, 1795-1880.* Kent: Kent State University, 1879, 1988. In 1827 John Malvin migrated from Virginia to Ohio.

Oklahoma
Burton, Art T. "Black Troops and the Battle of Honey Springs," *The Frontier Freedman's Journal* 1 no. 2 (1992).

Johnson, Hannibal B. *Black Wall Street: From Riot to Renaissance in Tulsa's Historic Greenwood District.* Austin: Eakin Press, 1998.

Pennsylvania
Carter, Alice Roster. *Can I Get a Witness? Growing Up in the Black Middle Class in Erie, Pennsylvania.* Erie: Erie County Historical Society, 1991.

Cole, Bettie. *Their Story: The History of Blacks/African Americans in Sewickley & Edgeworth.* Sewickley: B. Cole, 2000.

Harris, Richard E. *Politics and Prejudice: A History of Chester (Pa.) Negroes.* Apache Junction: Relmo, 1991.

Hodge, Ruth E. *Guide to African American Resources at the Pennsylvania State Archives.* Harrisburg: Commonwealth of Pennsylvania, Pennsylvania Historical and Museum Commission, 2000.

Matthews, Harry Bradshaw. *Whence They Came: the Families of United States Colored Troops in Gettysburg, Pennsylvania, 1815-1871.* Roosevelt: Matthews Heritage Service, 1992.

Sharp, Priscilla Stone. *Langhorn and Mary: a 19th Century American Love Story.* Phoenix: Ambrosia Books, 2003.

South Carolina

Ball, Edward. *Slaves in the Family.* New York: Ballantine Books, 1999.

Gourdin, J. Raymond. *Voices From the Past: 104th Infantry Regiment, USCT, Colored Civil War Soldiers from South Carolina.* Bowie: Heritage Books, 1997.

Johnson, Michael P. and James L. Roark. *Black Masters: A Free Family of Color in the Old South.* New York: W.W. Norton, 1984. The life and times of the William Ellison family, who were African American slaveowners, is examined.

Littlefield, Daniel C. *Rice and Slaves: Ethnicity and the Slave Trade in Colonial South Carolina* (reprinted). Urbana: University of Illinois Press, 1991.

Matthews, Harry Bradshaw. *African American Genealogical Research: How To Trace Your Family History.* Baldwin: Matthews Heritage Service, 1992.

Wood, Peter H. *Black Majority: Negroes in Colonial South Carolina from 1670 through the Stono Rebellion* (revised). New York: Norton, W.W., 1996.

Tennessee

Brasfield, Curtis. "To my daughter and the heirs of her body': Slave Passages as illustrated by the Latham Smithwick Family," *National Genealogical Society Quarterly* 81 no. 4 (December 1993). Model study.

Craighead, Sandra G. "Abstracts from *The Colored Tennessean* 1865-1867: Want Ads for Lost Relatives," *Journal of the Afro-American Historical and Genealogical Society* 12 nos. 3 & 4 (1991).

Texas

Crouch, Barry A. "Freedmen's Bureau Records: Texas, A Case Study". In *Afro-American History: Sources for Research*, pp. 74-97. Edited by Robert L. Clarke. Washington, DC: Howard University, 1981. Discusses former slaves' quest for family members.

Virginia/West Virginia

Cerny, Johni. "From Maria to Bill Cosby: A Case Study in Tracing Black Slave Ancestry. *National Genealogical Society Quarterly* 75 no. 1 (March 1987).

Griffith, Alvah H. *Pittsylvania County, Virginia Register of Free Negroes and Related Documentation*. Bowie, Heritage Books, 2001.

Smith, Gloria L. *Black Americans at Mount Vernon: Genealogy Techniques for Slave Group Research*. Tuscon: G.L. Smith, 1984.

Sutton, Karen E. *The Nickens Family: How To Trace a Non-slave African-American Lineage from Virginia to Maryland and Back*. Baltimore: KE Sutton, 1993.

——. "Nonwhite Soldiers and Sailors of the American Revolution from the Northern Neck of Virginia," *Flower of the Forest Black Genealogical Journal* 2 no. 3 (1996).

Wisconsin

Zachary, Cooper. *Black Settlers in Rural Wisconsin*. Madison, State Historical Society of Wisconsin, 1994.

Periodicals

Numerous indexing and abstracting services exist. The *Periodical Source Index* (PERSI) published by the Allen County Library Foundation for example, is a helpful resource for general genealogical newsletters and journals and should be consulted. *The Genealogical Periodical Annual Index* (GPAI) also has provided coverage genealogical periodicals. Some southern states have published indexes for statewide genealogical publications.

African American Coal Mining Heritage. Published by Timothy Pinnick, 206 Briar Lane, North Aurora, IL 60542. (vol. 1, 2004 —). Focuses upon coal mining culture and industry. E-mail: BLACKMINERS@YAHOO.COM Available through subscription.

Ebony. Chicago: Johnson Publishing.

Flower of the Forest: Black Genealogical Journal. Published by Agnes Kane Callum, Baltimore, Maryland. (vol. 1, no. 1 1982 – vol. 2, no. 16). Articles emphasize research in Maryland and Virginia. (out of print)

Frontier Freedman's Journal: An African American Genealogy Journal of Indian Territory and the West. Published by Angela Y. Walton-Raji, 6508 Woodbridge Circle, Baltimore, Maryland 21228. (vol. 1, no. 1 1992 – vol. 4, no. 1). Articles focus upon Arkansas and Oklahoma. (out of print).

International Sons and Daughters of Slave Ancestry Newsletter. Published by the International Sons and Daughters of Slave Ancestry, P.O. Box 436937, 2134 W. 95th Street, Chicago, Illinois 60643-6937. (vol. 1, no. 1 1988—) Subscription is available with annual dues.

Jersey Heritage. Published by the New Jersey Chapter, Afro-American Historical and Genealogical Society, P.O. Box 237, Jersey City, New Jersey 07303. (vol. 1, no. 1 1992 —).

Journal of the Afro-American Historical and Genealogical Society. Published semiannually by the Afro-American Historical and Genealogical Society, P.O. Box 73086, Washington, DC 20056-3086. (vol. 1, 1980 —). International scope. Subscription is available with annual dues. An index spanning from 1980 to 1990 is available (see listing under A, B, C's of Genealogy).

Journal of Negro History. Published by the Association for the Study of Afro-American History and Life, Washington, DC. Family histories have appeared.

Patricia Liddell Researcher News Journal. Published by the Patricia Liddell Researchers, Chicago Chapter AAHGS, Inc., P.O. Box 438652, Chicago, IL 60643. (vol. 1, 1993 —).

USCT Civil War Digest. Published semiannually by the United States Colored Troops Institute for Local History and Family Research, Associate Dean/USCT Institute, Center for Interdependence, Hartwick College, Oneonta, New York 13820. (vol. 1, no. 1 1999 —). Subscription is available with annual dues.

Media

Alex Haley: The Search for Roots. WNET-TV, 1977, 18 min., sd., col., 16 mm. Interview with Alex Haley about the research for *Roots.*

Black Studies. University of Arizona, 1980, tape, 60 min., b&w, ½ in. A series of 5 programs highlights the roots of Black Americans.

Cousins. Blackwood Films, 58 min., col., 16 mm. The story of the Vaughan family, now numbering more than several thousand, recounts the family's journey back through slavery in South Carolina to Nigeria.

Jacksons, The Moving On. Family Roots-You Be The Historian. GLOBEF. 1979, 45 fr., col., with cassette. Recounts how to use source documents to establish a family's migration, as a Black youth interviews his grandfather and traces three generations.

About the Author

Roland Barksdale-Hall, founder of the Afro-American Historical and Genealogical Society (AAHGS) of Pittsburgh and executive director, has been researching the black family for more than 25 years. In 2004 he hosted a three-day healing family gathering, entitled "The Restoration of the Family." His research resulted in the Millennium Family Reunion, held in Detroit, bringing together more than 300  descendants of enslaved African ancestors. He has signed entries on the "Black Family in the Colonial Era" and "Inheritance and Slave Status" in the *African-American History Reference Series*, edited by Paul Finkelman (Oxford University Press, 2005). His intriguing family history has been showcased in an exhibition, "From Color To Culture" in New York. He is the recipient of the prestigious 2003 Afro-American Historical and Genealogical Society (AAHGS) National History Award and the former Peabody Special Collection Librarian, Hampton University, Hampton, Virginia.

He currently serves as president of JAH Kente International, Inc. and vice president of Black Men for Progress. He is the director of the Mercer County Junior Frontiers. He has served as the vice president of *The Buckeye* Review and on the executive committee of the Black Caucus of the American Library Association, Inc. Other professional memberships include International Sons and Daughters of Slave Ancestry, National Association of Black Storytellers and Mercer County Historical Society. His family is the recipient of the 2001 Women in Ministry Shenango Valley Christian Family Award.

ORDER FORM

WWW.AMBERBOOKS.COM
African-American Self Help and Career Books

Fax Orders: 480-283-0991
Telephone Orders: 480-460-1660
Online Orders: E-mail: Amberbks@aol.com

Postal Orders: Send Checks & Money Orders to:
Amber Books Publishing
1334 E. Chandler Blvd., Suite 5-D67
Phoenix, AZ 85048

_____ *The African-American Family's Guide to Tracing Our Roots*
_____ *Langhorn and Mary*
_____ *Beside Every Great Man…Is A Great Woman*
_____ *How to Be an Entrepreneur and Keep Your Sanity*
_____ *The African-American Guide to Real Estate Investing, $30,000 in 30 Days*
_____ *The African-American Writer's Guide to Successful Self-Publishing*
_____ *Fighting for Your Life*
_____ *How to Get Rich When You Ain't Got Nothing*
_____ *Urban Suicide: The Enemy We Choose Not to See*
_____ *The African-American Job Seeker's Guide to Successful Employment*
_____ *The African-American Teenagers Guide to Personal Growth, Health, Safety, Sex and Survival*

Name:_____

Company Name:_____

Address:_____

City:_____State:_____Zip:_____

Telephone: (_____) _____E-mail:_____

For Bulk Rates Call: **480-460-1660**   **ORDER NOW**

Tracing Our Roots	$14.95	❑ Check ❑ Money Order ❑ Cashiers Check
Langhorn & Mary	$25.95	❑ Credit Card: ❑ MC ❑ Visa ❑ Amex ❑ Discover
Beside Every Great Man	$14.95	
How to be an Entrepreneur	$14.95	CC#_____
Real Estate Investing	$14.95	
Successful Self-Publishing	$14.95	Expiration Date:_____
Fighting for Your Life	$14.95	**Payable to:** Amber Books
How to Get Rich	$14.95	1334 E. Chandler Blvd., Suite 5-D67
Urban Suicide	$14.95	Phoenix, AZ 85048
Job Seeker's Guide	$14.95	
Teenagers Guide	$19.95	**Shipping:** $5.00 per book. Allow 7 days for delivery.

Shipping: $5.00 per book. Allow 7 days for delivery.
Sales Tax: Add 7.05% to books shipped to
Arizona addresses.
Total enclosed: $_____